COLONIALISM AND CHRISTIAN MISSION: POSTCOLONIAL REFLECTIONS

COLONIALISM AND CHRISTIAN MISSION: POSTCOLONIAL REFLECTIONS

Jacob S. Dharmaraj

ISPCK
1993

Colonialism and Christian Mission: Postcolonial Reflections—Published by the Indian Society for Promoting Christian Knowledge (ISPCK), Post Box 1585, Kashmere Gate, Delhi-110 006.

Price: Rs. 75.00

ISBN 81-7214-114-9

Typeset by Imprint, 16 North Avenue, Punjabi Bagh, Delhi-110 026.

Printed at Cambridge Press, Kashmere Gate, Delhi-110 006.

To Glory, my wife

Contents

Contents

Foreword and Acknowledgements

The purpose of this book is mainly to explore the nineteenth century European missiological thought and missionary method of the British mission societies to India. The investigation primarily centers around selected missionaries like William Carey and Alexendar Duff. The project examines how mission societies worked in close association with colonial power in carrying out missionary work in India.

Without, in any way, minimizing the monumental contribution the missionaries and the mission societies have made to the furtherance of the Gospel, this book presents a "rereading" of the dominant colonial missiological facts in order to bring out the subordinate voice of the politically colonized Indians.

The book presents the centrist/marginal paradigm of the nineteenth century European missiological enterprise. The work reclaims the silenced, colonized view point through a background study of British mission societies and colonial connections. The study deals with the workings of the colonial epistemology, colonial missiography, the identity of the colonized, and the rise of nationalist politics.

I have undertaken this project since concepts of postcolonialism as a methodology have not be adequately utilized. I hesitantly provide what has been lacking in the act of historicizing mission enterprises.

Several people have helped and encouraged me in the years I spent in academic study and ministry. It is impossible for me even to attempt to mention all the professors and friends in academy who have helped me to learn of mission and Christian history; who have enabled me in shaping and formulating my thought. Of particular assistance in preparing this project were the following:

Professor James A. Scherer, Professor of World Mission at the Lutheran School of Theology at Chicago, who directed my doctoral work in mission history. He has been a source of inspiration ever since I started graduate studies in Chicago. Professor Scherer's critical remarks and suggestions were essential to the formation of this work. He has graciously consented to write the preface for this book.

Ms. Cynthia Echols, a friend of our family, for her skillful editorial work which has made the manuscript more readable than it would have been otherwise. Her daughter, Nichole Echols, brought immense joy and happiness during my years of struggle in Chicago.

Dr. James Massey and Mr. Ashish Amos of ISPCK for their timely help in preparing the manuscript for publication.

My wife, Glory. I would never have undertaken or completed my doctoral studies without the unfailing sympathy and constant encouragement of my wife. I would never have completed this work without the patience and inspiration of my wife. I am grateful to her.

J.S. Dharmaraj

Preface

History from the Underside

The point of J.S. Dharmaraj's "post-colonial reflections" on colonialism and nineteenth century Christian missions in India is to give history back to those who passively experienced it: the people of India. This is history written from "the underside", i.e. from the point of view of its victims. As an exercise in historical revisionism, it seeks to give new meaning and to offer a new understanding of events which until now have been viewed mainly from "the top down", i.e. from the standpoint of colonial masters.

Employing the now widely used technique of structural criticism, the author shows how glowing reports of the successes of the evangical missionary movement in combating idolatry and cultural backwardness in India during the first half of the nineteenth century were laden with western cultural assumptions which did not get to the heart of the matter. These reports reflected an evangelical triumphalism born of imperial grandeur, a mixture of British patriotism and evangelical fervor. Dharmaraj does not for a moment doubt the sincerity of the writers of those glowing missionary accounts, but he maintains that they were not aware of their own hidden ideological assumptions. Caught up by the mystique of the imperial cause, they did not realize that religion was not a neutral commodity, or the extent to which missionary activities fully shared in the wider context by which British hegemony was imposed on the people of colonial India.

A leading theme is that the textual accounts by evangelical advocates documented in this work more accurately reflect the culture and psyche, the motives and aspirations of the British evangelical community of the nineteenth century than the reality of India. Structural criticism attempts to break down the total phenomenon of colonial overlordship into its separate social, economic, political, cultural and educational components so as to disclose the manner in which the Christian religion functioned within the system. Any account of evangelical missionary work which does not clearly demonstrate western religion's compliance with the entire colonial edifice, the author believes, cannot serve the needs of the Indian people for an unbiased account. The method of structural analysis bears some resemblance to the Marxist view of religion as part of the ideological superstructure which protects the economic infrastructure, but it is more comprehensive and thorough-going than the Marxist approach.

This revisionist approach to colonial history tends to see the people of India, and more particularly its ongoing Christian community, more as unwilling participants in an enterprise controlled from abroad, rather than as actual makers of their own destinies. Such an interpretation raises many interesting questions, and opens up new vistas for interpretation, which are only partly explored in the present work. If it is the case that such knowledge and discernment bestows freedom from past limitations, yields fresh vision, or enables new undertakings, then what is the practical value of this intelligence? How does structural analysis clarify the life situation of Indian Christian converts—both then and now? What practical difference does it make?

Will recognition that the Indian Christian community originated in part as a captive and colonized community act as a liberating and energizing force for that community today, or will it only serve to further paralyze and rationalize the community's responses? Employing the gift of hindsight, the author regrets that the evangelical missionary movement from Britain in the nineteenth century did not assume more of the character of a "liberation movement". Regrettably, the theology of liberation was not an available option at that time. But can the delayed recognition of the operating force of the gospel, authentically proclaimed, work its liberating operation on the people of India today? Can the Christian community in India gain a new identity from the gospel message of freedom, and how will that identity be put to use? One senses here an immediate link with the emerging "Dalit theology" movement in India.

A host of other questions are triggered by the author's "post-colonial reflections". How does the post-colonial Christian identity relate to other Christian communities (including the former colonial masters) within the global *oikoumene*? What is its relation to the other dominant religious communities of India? Does the new post-colonial identity give Indian Christians a mandate to play a renewed prophetic role, as was the case in the troubled times after Indian independence? Will the new identity intensify and galvanize existing movements toward Christian unity? Among the most challenging of these unanswered questions is whether the recovery (or rediscovery) of a lost identity by Indian Christians will lead to a deepened conviction about the mission and purpose of the Indian Christian community.

Dr. Dharmaraj is to be congratulated on his serious attempt to view Indian Christian history from the perspective of contemporary Indian national history, statehood, and multi-culturality. He should be encouraged to carry forward his investigations into the character of Indian Christianity so as to permit them to disclose their deeper implications for the mission of the Indian church.

James A. Scherer, Th.D.
Chicago, Illinois, USA

Introduction

I begin this book with a story—a borrowed story from another continent—reflecting a shared colonial experience:

> There was a little boy in an African village who customarily came home from the mission school with excitement about his learning of the day. On one particular day, he came home with a look of puzzlement on his face. And when he came into his house his father inquired about his puzzlement. The little boy said, "Father, I don't understand this. I go to school everyday and the teacher often tells us the story about this lion who they say is the king of the jungle. But this ferocious and strong beast always seems to get killed by the hunter in the story. I don't understand it. If the lion is so strong, why does the hunter always kill the lion?" The father responded, "Well, son, until lions learn how to write books, that's the way the story will always end."[1]

My project in this book is an attempt to analyze the reported events of the European mission to India in the nineteenth and early twentieth centuries from the "unrepresented"– heretofore unexpressed – "colonized perspective." I believe that the story of Christian mission, like the fictive lion's story, lends itself to a "reading" and a "counter-reading"; that is, a traditionalist Western interpretation and a rereading from a colonized viewpoint. What I attempt to bring out in this book is a reconsideration and rewriting of part of the European Christian mission history of India in the nineteenth and twentieth centuries from the "lion's" perspective.

During the above-mentioned period, the church of Jesus Christ was established in almost all corners of the world, particularly in the colonized world. Since most countries were colonized by Protestant Christian Europe, the occupied lands saw a proliferation

---

1. Story quoted by Jacquelyn Grant in *The Kairos Covenant,* ed., Wills H. Logan (New York: Friendship Press, 1988), p. 131.

of Protestant mission societies and a rapid multiplication of evangelical missionaries. Colonizers and missionaries sailed on the same boat; gun and gospel were carried on the same ship.

Under the pretext of civilizing and modernizing the colonized lands after the model of Europe, the conquerors expanded their territories around the world, particularly in India. The missionaries subscribed to the view that "civilizing" the Indian people would prepare the "primitive religious people" to embrace Christianity. In the nineteenth century, Christianization and civilization were considered two sides of the same coin. Therefore, European colonization was politically justified and missiologically encouraged. Conversion of soul and conquest of the body bore the same spiritual stamp. All the European mission societies agreed in principle that colonization of India was the divine providence, and that it was the moral duty of the colonizers and spiritual commitment of the missionaries to civilize and Christianize the natives. Anyone or anything that stood in the way of civilizing and converting the people of India was vehemently opposed. The Muslims, the Brahmins, and their religious beliefs were considered impediments to mission and colonization progress.

The Indian people's social and religious life was portrayed as culturally inferior, intellectually backward, and religiously superstitious. Indian cultural life was seen as archaic, inefficient, and static. As a subcontinent India, therefore, had to be dusted, disinfected, and injected with a western style of education, jurisprudence, and religion. This rationalization of social institutions was seen as a precondition for the introduction of Christianity.

The dual emphasis of European patriotism and Christian mission generated enthusiasm in the West, and continued to foster in European minds the binary task of civilizing and missionizing colonized India. Hence the rationally motivated social activity was strongly recommended both to strategically introduce Christian faith and to break the spell of Indian religious faiths. In their attempt to introduce Christianity strategically, the mission societies gave the communicative action of the gospel and the demonstrative dynamic of the Christian power secondary place. The normative belief in European racial and cultural superiority was perpetuated until India's independence in 1947.

The precursor to communication is understanding. The forerunner to testimony is acceptance. A superimposed religious faith cannot be counted subjectively as the acceptance of a belief or the understanding of the receiving subjects.[2] The predicament of colonized people in India during the nineteenth century was one of sorrow, grief, and helplessness.

In this book I examine the relationship that existed between the colonizers and the colonized, and between the purpose of European Christian mission to India in the nineteenth and twentieth centuries and the wider colonial structure of which it was a part. More specifically, I intend to apply a post-colonial perspective in order to analyze the missiological principles of William Carey and Alexander Duff, the two outstanding missionaries of the above era, and their association with colonial institutions.

Carey's relation to colonial economic structure has not been fully explored from a post-colonial monetary viewpoint. The interplay of colonial economy and European missionaries in the administration of Indian ecclesiastical structure, which was made up of native converts, has been riddled with colonial irony, monetary injustice, and economic disparity. This economic injustice, which was in practice consciously or unconsciously within the mission structure during the colonial era, is not completely absent in Western mission involvement in developing societies even today.

Duff's introduction of English education in India within the colonial parameters and missiological enterprise promoted the undervaluation of Indian culture. His failure to consider Eastern culture in the broader perspective of a theology of creation and his employment of a methodology which let European cultural and political values precede biblical and missiological principles helped formulate a context for mission which was existential in dimension. This alliance between European mission and hegemonic imposition of Western education has not been adequately examined.

My argument is that the patterns of nineteenth-century colonial mission were linked to European colonizers' social and political vicissitudes, as well as to certain relatively invariable aspects of European political and cultural traditions. The interplay of European cultural, political and missiological factors illuminates

---

2. See J. Habermas, *The Theory of Communicative Action: Reason and the Rationalization of Society*, tr. T. McCarthy, (Boston: Beaver Press, 1984).

how educational, judicial, religious, and ecclesiastical systems in India underwent major transformations, and still retained various national and cultural features. Thus while the colonial, administrative, and missiological structure had enveloped the exteriority of the manifested, colonized public system, the interior, subterranean undercurrent of the Indian people's everyday life retained all of its indigenous, original orientation.

Unwilling to understand the complexities of Indian cultural variants and deeply entrenched in their transcendent belief in the Western scientific approach to people of other cultures and religious faith, the European missionaries and English colonial administrators asserted that Hinduism and animism would die away soon, and that the whole nation could be civilized and Christianized with the introduction of English education.

Broadly speaking, the missionaries could not understand how the people of India would adopt a seemingly contradictory colonized stance. With their long historical, religious background, Indians would externally adopt European values in education, science, and technology. At the same time, they would conform to the exigencies of Indian religious life which in its entirety was diametrically opposed to Western cultural values. This double aspect of the Indian psyche has been at home for centuries within a dialectically opposed and diametrically conflictive Eastern cultural and religious duality which remains a baffling mystery to empirically oriented Westerners even today.

The cultural compartmentalization, and the complex and variegated relationship between conscious and metaphysical realities, indicate that the colonial, political, administrative and missiological methodologies failed to make a successful inroad on the consciousness of the Indian people whom the English dominated for two centuries.

Using the methodologies of Michel Foucault, Edward Said, and Raymond Schwab, I treat colonial mission as a discourse and a structure of evangelistic beliefs, and as part of European cultural practices that reflected the colonists' political, economic and cultural manifestation. I posit nineteenth and twentieth-century European mission history as a movement having ideological and practical colonial functions. In that process, I deal with the hermeneutics of mission in broad post-colonial terms, and with

its missiological principles in a wider, imperialist and epistemological narrative structure.

My argument is not to say or prove that the colonial Christian
mission to India was nothing but a bunch of lies or distorted
evangelistic fact. Rather, colonial mission was an outcome of the
eighteenth-century evangelical revival which gave birth to the
Evangelical Party in the Church of England and to the
multiplication of the new denominations of Wesleyan and
Calvinistic Methodism, an integral part of the colonial political
structure and the accumulated result of Western cultural practice.
I see the domineering European political structure in India on
the one hand, and the colonial evangelistic theology on the other,
as a single constitutive reality. Attempting to separate colonial
ideology from missionary theology, or colonial hermeneutics from
a mission model and its epistemological methodologies in
evangelistic action, would be futile. Since this kind of functional
relationship between colonialism and mission spanned the
nineteenth century, mission and colonialism in effect favored
and facilitated each other and helped carry out certain ideologies
over others.

My treatment of colonial mission literatures is focussed on
functional aspects that were regarded, accepted, and understood
by a vast majority of European mission historians. My interest
in the external and representational areas of mission stems from
the methodological and theoretical considerations being practiced
by the missionaries during the colonial period. In my theoretical
consideration, I regard the colonial mission to be primarily a
cultural, political, and missiological phenomenon expressing
European collective ideas and the colonizers' administrative and
political practices, rather than something which was expressed
only as a pure, visionary reflection of the natural, spontaneous
movement of the Wesleyan revival in the eighteenth century. My
work, primarily, covers from 1833 to 1947. I do, however, deal
briefly with the evangelistic work of William Carey, which goes
back to the beginning of the nineteenth century.

In summary, my argument is that nineteenth and early
twentieth-century European Christian mission to India was a
cultural and missiological fact. European missionary awakening
had indisputable connections with colonial expansion. During
the colonial era, the church in England was hardly interested in

those of whom it had essentially heard nothing, either through the reports of colonizers or adventures of travellers. Since its evangelistic principles had both colonial and ecclesiastical underpinnings, the colonial mission was, to borrow Said's terminology, both "circumstantial" and "worldly."

CHAPTER I

Modern Historiography

Christian mission constantly has to wrestle with the question of handling the "other," dealing with the issue of difference, and ministering to people of diverse background. In the last fifty years, Christian theologians have come up with concepts such as indigenization, inculturation, contextualization, and internalization of the good news of the Bible, and numerous books have been written on these notions. A comprehensive and historicized understanding of the other in relation to the self's missionizing efforts of that other has not yet been achieved. This lack only perpetuates the urgent requisite for understanding God and his creation as we gain more knowledge, and the compelling need for discerning human history under a new light by each succeeding generation.

In his book *Altarity* Mark Taylor talks about the suppression of minority voices by the dominant forces. He deals with "the undeniably political urgency of the issue of difference." Taylor suggests that the systematic exclusion of the significance of difference seen in the other will undoubtedly result in the politics of appropriation and domination. Taylor analyzes how the other's voice has been silenced by dominant culture, and raises pertinent questions about handling the other.

The history of society and culture is, in large measure, a history of struggle with the endlessly complex problems of difference and otherness. Never have the questions posed by difference and otherness been more pressing than they are today. For an era dominated by the struggle between, among, and against various "isms"—communism, fascism, totalitarianism, capitalism, racism, sexism etc.,—the issue of difference is undeniably political. Is difference tolerable? Are others to be encouraged to express and cultivate their differences? Or is difference intolerable? Are others who are different to be converted, integrated, dominated, excluded, or repressed?[3]

---

3. Mark Taylor, *Altarity*, (Chicago: University of Chicago Press, 1987), p. xxi.

However noble its goal, profound its theoretical material, sincere its deliberation, and poignant its historical documents, the written history of nineteenth-century colonial Christian mission has been predicated on various themes of value subordination of ancient cultures, and socio-religious conversion of the colonized people. Subordination provided control over the silenced subjects, while conversion reconstructed values through their subsumption into yet new principles of unity.

Concurring with this notion, Martha Nussbaum in *Fragility of Goodness* says that by discounting the moral values of the other, the other can be appropriated and justice denied. "To do justice to the nature or identity of two distinct values requires doing justice to their difference – both their qualitative distinctness and their numerical separateness – requires seeing that there are, at least potentially, circumstances in which the two will collide. Distinctness requires articulation from, bounding-off against. This, in turn, entails the possibility of opposition – and for the agent who is committed to both – of conflict."[4]

The mission historians of the nineteenth century devalued the social, religious, and cultural values of the colonized East, and wrote history from European imperialistic, colonial, and political perspectives. As a result their written documents must be reexamined from post-colonial Indian perspectives.

After the independence of India in 1947, Indian secular historians insisted that the political and cultural history of India should be rewritten by the natives themselves. As a result, R.C.Majumdar and his associates labored for over ten years to write volumes on Indian political and social history. In the same vein, Indian church historians felt the scholarly need to rewrite Indian Christian history, and have produced several volumes with the encouragement of the Church History Association of India.

The Indian Christian historians recognize the total inadequacy and cultural bias of the European intellectual tradition in its attempt to provide the Indian church with Christian, universal, conceptual and religious norms. Hence, the Indian Christian

---

4. Martha Nussbaum, *Fragility of Goodness,* (Cambridge/New York: Cambridge University Press, 1986), p.68.

scholars insist that the native church must cut herself off from the cultural, theological, and spiritual moorings of Western triumphalism, and build a healthy, disciplined skepticism regarding Western appropriation of Indian church and her historic past.

The writers of Indian church history are increasingly turning their attention to the colonial period and the subordinated knowledge of the colonized. These historians demonstrate the scholarly necessity of what Michel Foucault refers to as an "insurrection of subjugated knowledge." In other words, examination of the written documents from the perspective of the silenced voice of the colonized is undertaken as a native historian's task. Evidently that quest must be conducted in the light of the new identity Indian Christians have found in the post-independent India, and with genuine appreciation for all the good things the European mission societies have done to benefit the people of India.

In my search for the European missionary motive, I recognized that European historiography has been tainted by colonial epistemology and a racist hermeneutic that reinforced the superiority of European culture and the normative character of English education as the sole arbitrator of Christian tradition. The distortion of truth can be confronted only through critical analyses of written documents and by unearthing the "archaeology of knowledge" constructed by European scholars. Hence in this book I speak as a post-colonial subject and attempt to bring out the "buried" and "subjugated" knowledge of the native other which exists as an object.[5]

Since the end of World War II, the advent of modern technologies and fundamental changes in political, social, and economic structures have altered the intellectual attitudes and modified the foundations of traditional historiography. Traditional historiography has gone through complex changes, particularly in the areas of theory-building and quantification. World War II brought about the destruction of the social and political monopoly of the European West in the colonized East.

The emerging nations achieved national consciousness, and

---

5. Michel Foucault, *Power/Knowledge,* trans. Colin Gordon, (Brighton, Sussex: Harvester Press, 1980), p. 80,81.

began to look at their past from a different perspective. The romantic, optimistic history of civilization was replaced by disillusionment. Modern civilization and advanced technological societies were seen as potentially destructive forces.

Human history was reviewed in a different light by a group of European thinkers such as Max Weber, Theodore Lassing, Karl Popper, Claude Levi-Strauss, and Michel Foucault. They proposed alternative modes of interpreting history. For instance, Foucault placed much emphasis on a reading which takes into consideration the discontinuities and ruptures in history. Lèvi-Strauss, contrary to Treitschke's bold declaration that "Men make history,"[6] argues that the conception of the "historical process as a continuous development" is "fallacious" and "contradictory."[7] He assigns a greater significance to the "substratum of history." Forces outside human consciousness and control, especially economic or social factors and psychological, anthropological and linguistic structures were assigned a decisive significance for an understanding of history.

To these thinkers, history is a reality-seeking enterprise. They propose that a closer relationship has to be established between the phenomena of consciousness and their sources in the subconscious. Events have to be understood in the structural context in which they occurred. Pure narration is insufficient, and it has to be supplemented by analysis. Politics alone is no longer the keystone to history. Politics interacting with socio-economic-cultural factors should be accounted for and analyzed in order to understand history properly. In short, the non-political spheres ought to be searched and investigated to understand history.

In this vein Foucault proposes in *The Archaeology of Knowledge* to study history as part of an archive, a text which is composed of discourses, which in turn are made of statements. He treats history as part of a cultural diffusion; a close-knit system which is hard to penetrate. He argues that everything stated in a particular

6. Fernand Brandel, *On History*, trans. by Sarah Matthews, (Chicago: The University of Chicago Press, 1980), p. 10.
7. Claude Lèvi-Strauss, *The Savage Mind*, (Chicago: The University of Chicago Press, 1966), p. 260.
8. Foucault, *The Archaeology of Knowledge*, pp. 79-131.

field, for example literary history or medical discourse, is produced only with the most selective method; one strand of thought is preferred over the other.[8] Therefore, each statement in the text is a material effort to incorporate a particular piece of reality as selectively as possible. My final chapter explains how such selective methods were adapted by the Mills, the Trevelyans and Macaulay when Indian culture and people were assessed in the scale of civilization and the principles of reformation were introduced.

While Foucault places the text's situation in the world of culture, Raymond Schwab in *The Oriental Renaissance* proposes that texts are the result of an encounter between familiar and novel ideas; yet such an encounter is eminently circumstantial and material. He contends that texts are produced in time and in society by human beings who are themselves agents of their actual history.[9] Schwab and Foucault have gone very far in determining the social and external factors that operate upon production of texts, as well as the discursive and cultural systems within which texts are produced. And hence, they suggest, it is important for historians to find out the "archive" of the time and the strategic combinations in which power and knowledge occur and make it possible for the texts to circulate. In short, we have to see history not as a solitary object existing independent of any context.

History is not an autonomous entity; it is rather an unconscious expression of collective forces like culture, power, value systems and dominant thoughts. And so it is the challenge of the critical historian to determine when history is said to be a voluntary expression of community, where history has intertwined with external surroundings, and how history has represented the dominant thought of its time.

One way of determining history is to view it as a "dynamic field" as Said does.

> History has a certain range of reference, a system of tentacles partly potential, partly actual; to the author, to the reader, to a historical situation, to other texts, to the past and present. In another sense no text is finished, since its potential

9. Raymond Scwab, *The Oriental Renaissance,* (Paris: Payot, 1950).
10. Edward Said, *The World, the Text and the Critic* (Cambridge, Mass.: Harvard University Press, 1933), p.11.

range is always being extended by every additional reader.
Now the critic's task is obviously first to understand how
the text was and is made. No details are too trivial, provided
one's study is directed carefully toward the text as a vital
aesthetic and cultural whole.[10]

An examination of nineteenth-century missionary work in
India requires an analysis of the mission work and its literatures
and a reconstruction of the dominant political structure of that
period in order to interpret history against its backdrop of events.
As I have posited in the Introduction, nineteenth-century colonial
mission was a cultural, political, and missiological fact. The
literatures it produced do not exist independent of any external
constraints. The mission texts, like any other literatures, were
influenced by the dominant external political, cultural, and
economic factors, which Said calls "the facts of textuality."[11]

The missionaries were able to carry out their work in India
due to colonial monetrism and the Evangelicals' political activism.[12]
As much as Carey and his colleagues were kept away from British
India during the early phase of their missionary careers by the
Charter Act of 1793, never would they have carried out the
Serampore mission successfully without the help and cooperation
of the British administrators and the colonial expansionists. The
enormous amount of money Carey received as salary from the
indigo planters, and the huge amount of money he was paid by
the British Administrative government in Bengal in exchange
for training colonial administrators to govern India at Fort William
College, are just a few examples I will cite at this point.[13] The
same holds true for John Wilson, Alexander Duff, and several
other missionaries and their close association with the government
and colonizers in carrying out their missions. As for the mission
societies, the proliferation of mission stations in and around
Calcutta, the power center of the colonial government, after the
Charter was renewed in 1833, speaks for itself.[14]

---

11. Edward Said, *Orientalism* (New York: Basic Books, 1975), p. 13.
12. I shall explain the meaning of colonial monetrism in Chapter IV.
13. I deal with the exploitation of the indigo planters and how much William
Carey was paid as a supervisor in Chapter III.
14. I deal in more detail with each of the above missionaries and the societies
and their association with the British administrators in subseqent sections.

Commenting on the above-mentioned period of mission history, twentieth-century mission historians such as Kenneth Scott Latourette, Stephen Neill, and several others, like their nineteenth-century counterparts, continue to believe in the presence of God in Indian history and "the miraculous subjugation" of the country by a handful of Europeans.[15] Since the country was brought under European rule with such ease, the Western mission scholars continued to justify the surrogate parenthood assumed by the politicians, colonial administrators, plantation managers, and missionaries in order to mold the shape and course of colonized India's history.

However, what they refused to take into account was the oppressive political, military and cultural measures which were appropriated by the administrators and the expansionists. Those measures were solely responsible for bringing the country under the Europeans, and it was this structure that aided the mission societies in their work among the people of India. Through this refusal to look into the explicit connection between missionary work and colonial exploitations, European historians attempt to keep the missionary work and the mission literatures from being criticized.

Colonization contributed to the intentional prevarication of the policies of the expansionists through manipulation, terror, and war. Missionary work in India was the intentional product of eighteenth-century evangelicalism and European patriotism. The focus of the twentieth-century Western mission historians often ignores the mission's political aspect, or the "power and knowledge" relations between the colonizers and the missionaries.[16] This aspect would remain as the center of my analysis of the mission literatures.

Missionary ideology of the last century did not differ from the hegemonic ideology of the nineteenth century in its dependence

---

15. William Campell points out that the missionaries and directors of the East India Company were convinced of the divine intervention in favor of the Company; the conquest of India was a divine sanction, designed and adapted to become an inestimable blessing to the natives, by its becoming the means of the gradual introduction of Christianity. William Campell, *British India,* (London: John Snow, 1939), pp. 24-25.
16. See Michel Foucault, *Power/Knowledge,* pp. 80ff.

upon the production and consumption of signs, or what we might call the evangelistic economy. In order to understand this missiological relationship, we must examine the relationship between the colonizers and missionaries, and the policies and doctrines of nineteenth-century British India.

Another important factor one should bear in mind in the study of nineteenth-century mission literature is the conscious nineteenth-century European attitude toward the people of India: European culture is advanced, modern, and rational;[17] whereas, Indian culture is backward, archaic, and superstitious.[18]

Furthermore, Political and missiological work in nineteenth-century India was grounded in the binary distinction fostered by the philologists and orientalists: European and Indian, white and brown, civilized and primitive, and Christian and pagan. The binary division gave colonizers justifiable grounds and legitimate rights to present to the European public why the Indian subcontinent should be brought under European sovereignty and the natives subjugated under Western cultural order.

India should be conquered because it belonged "outside." Its religion is "abominable," its morality low, and its living standard uncultured. Indians were perceived as lazy, ignorant, and uncivilized and so they must be converted and civilized. They were considered as human material. They were perceived as tools. They were invisible humans.[19] Hence the Europeans, during the nineteenth century had a simple goal: the people in India should be converted, changed and transformed from outside to inside since they are not the self-same. They are the other.[20]

Modern mission historiography has created significant space

17. Eric Stokes, *The English Utilitarians and India* (Oxford: Clarendon Press, 1959), p.42.
18. See Denys Hay, *Europe: The Emergence of an Idea,* 2nd ed. (Edinburgh: Edinburgh University Press, 1968).
19. Thomas R. Metcalf, *The Aftermath of Revolt, — India, 1857-1870,* (Princeton, N.J. Princeton University Press, 1964), p. 10.
20. See Eugene Stock, *History of the Church Missionary Society,* (London: Gilbert and Rivington, 1899), Vol. IV, pp.24-101; Eric Stokes, *English Utilitarians in India,* pp. 34ff.; Charles Grant, *Observations on the State of Society among the Asiatic Subjects of Great Britain, particularly with respect to Moral and Means of Improving it,* (Privately Printed, 1972). pp. 220ff.; Metcalf, *Aftermath of Revolt,* p.8ff.

for the tragic event of the holocaust. If modern history has given such an importance to the tragic events of the holocaust, a recent past, then the Amritsar Massacre of 1923 – the iron-fist rule of the colonizers that created famine, poverty, mutiny and massacre in India – which were some of the tragic events of the distant past, should be given a textual space too. Since they have not been assigned a place in the mission texts, an appropriate place should be created. In order to do it, mission history has to be decolonized. A dehegemonized history thus will bring out the colonized East's muted history not as the other but as an alterity in its otherness. In other words, a historian's task is to enable the other to exist in its otherness without any reference to the self: the East on its own terms without reference to the West in its binary dependency.

Mission literatures were produced in an intellectual setting of British political and cultural imperialism. For instance, John Stuart Mill, Thomas Macaulay, Charles Trevelyan, and Karl Marx had set views on race and British administration in India. They made it explicit in their writings that they had to set a different standard for the people of India as they were civilizationally "inferior."[21]

The mission history has been written from the colonizers' point of view by the Europeans, who were visitors, missionaries, spectators, or supporters of Western hegemonic policies of the colonial rule.[22] Their philosophy of mission history has been constructed on the premise of India's abasement: the subordination of the nation to the Euro-evangelico-cultural order, which gives the appearance of being the condition for the machinery's functioning.

Now it has become rather urgent to question the solidarity between nineteenth-century hegemonism and Euro-centric evan-

21. Karl Marx, for example, in *The Eighteenth Brummaireof Louis Bonaparte*, writing about the incapacitated, vulnerable Asia, encouraged Europe to act as a surrogate self and wrote, "The East cannot represent itself, it should be represented." (Sie konnen sich nicht vertreten, sie mussen vertreten werden.) Quoted by Edward Said in *Orientalism*, p. 21.

22. For example, Stephen Neill's *The Cross over Asia* (London: The Canterbury Press, 1948) was written after his six weeks whirlwind tour across all Asia; K.S. Latourette wrote about India depending mainly on the documents written by European scholars for European readers.

gelical mission. It is a post-colonial imperative to challenge the stability of the European mission structure that passed itself off as eternal and natural. This de-Europeanizing or de-hegemonizing of the mission history will enable a historian to retell the history differently and provide a true representation of the people, culture, and history of colonized India. In other words, if we understand the prevailing cultural influence, the political and administrative doctrines, and so on, of nineteenth-century Europe and India, we can better understand the missionary work and its association with the colonial structure.

CHAPTER II

The Background of Nineteenth Century Mission

For Protestant Christianity, the nineteenth century was the missionary era *par excellence*[23] and "the Great Century"[24] for missions. The mission history written during this period was, in fact, written with an air of "romantic notion,"[25] a spirit of "triumphalism."[26] At times, the missionaries exaggerated their achievements and over-calculated their results. Concurrent with this view, David King says of the missionaries, "[The missionaries] over estimated their success, and in relation to the prospects of the missionary cause, allowed themselves to indulge in hopes which facts have not justified."[27]

In addition, nineteenth-century mission history, which is mostly the denominational history, was written from the European, colonizers' point of view. The mission societies considered the India mission, as echoed in the Edinburgh conference, "the domain of missions." Their goal in mission was not only to convert the heathens to Christianity but also to civilize them. While commenting on the motive of the European mission in the nineteenth century, Klaus Knorr observes, "Viewed in retrospect, its essence was an aggressive cultural imperialism, propaganda for the spread of European ideas and ideals over the face of the globe."[28]

Moreover, nineteenth-century India mission history lacks coherence and does not form a coherent whole. The mission work was carried out with the aid of European colonizers with a view to civilizing and Christianizing the people. Indian historians

---

23. Rober Adler, *Western Missions* (London: Longman, 1842), p. vi.

24. Kenneth S. Latourette, *History of the Expansion of Christianity*, vol. 5 (New York & London: Harper and Row Bros., 1943).

25. R.C. Moore, *Spread of Christianity* (Chicago: The University of Chicago, 1919), p.19.

26. See T.V. Philip, "Christianity in India During Western Colonialism: Conflict, Reconciliation, or Adjustment," *The Indian Church History Review* (Bangalore: The Church History Association of India, 1987), p. 16.

27. David King, *The State and Progress of Jamaica* (London, 1850), p. 130.

28. Klaus E. Knorr, *British Colonial Theories 1570-1850* (Toronto: University of Toronto Press, 1944), p. 381.

such as T.V. Philip and S.K. Das argue that the recorded mission history is incomplete, and that it has to be re-read and re-written from the post-colonial perspective.

An important point one has to keep in mind in understanding Indian church history is that the Indian church is made up of an insignificant number of people and that the church itself is a weak church with a feeble voice in a country inhabited by a vast majority of people of other faiths. The church thrived, and mass movements occurred in the last two centuries, mainly among the depressed caste people who lived far away from the urban centers in areas where the colonial government was not challenged by natives. Material benefits extended to the low-caste converts certainly did help the church achieve numerical growth.

Educated non-Christian, high-caste communities and people living in towns and cities mostly rejected the church and its mission work since they misconstrued the material help offered to the needy as an incentive to convert to the Christian faith. Moreover, they developed a wrong notion of associating Christianity with the religion only of oppressed communities. They condemned Christianity as a Western religion and accused it of being used as a means for the extension of Western political control over India. They substantiated their arguments with what the Portuguese did to the Muslims and Hindus on the West coast.

Their arguments were not without valid reason. The relationship between the colonizers and the colonized, between Europe and India, between missionaries and converts, was a relationship of power, of European covetousness, of domination, and of varying degrees of a complex hegemony.[29] The intellectuals and the leaders of the country argued that Christian work in India was being carried out to perpetuate the presence of the colonizers. The non-Christian Indian leaders were skeptical of the Christian message. Raja Ram Mohan Roy in 1821 expressed this suspicion when he asked the missionaries to do evangelistic work in non-colonized countries.

It is true that the apostles of Jesus Christ used to preach the superiority of Christian religion to the natives of different

---

29. See K.M. Panikkar, *Asia and Western Dominance* (London: George Allen & Urwin, 1959).

countries. But we must recollect they were not of the rulers of those countries where they preached. Were the missionaries likewise to preach the Gospel and distribute books in countries not conquered by the English such as Turkey, Persia etc., which are much nearer England, they would be esteemed as a body of men truly zealous in propagating religion and in following the example of the founders of Christianity. In Bengal, where the English are rulers, and where the mere name of English man is sufficient to frighten people, an encroachment upon the rights of her poor, timid and humble inhabitants and upon their religion, cannot be viewed in the eyes of God or the public as a justifiable act.[30]

To many citizens of India accepting Christianity and surrendering their religious faiths to this "foreign religion" would amount to an act of submission to colonial power. Chakkarai, a brahmin convert and a prominent lawyer from Madras, India, justified the fear of the caste Hindus when he asked, "Why should the Hindus who yielded in politics and commerce allow the sanctity of their souls to be violated by the intrusion of a foreign religious denomination?"[31] The Hindus who preserved their religious purity during Mogul domination and Portuguese invasion resolved to keep it that way even during British aggression.

In general, the argument of the Indian people was that the evangelization of India was being attempted not only because India was discovered to be pagan in all those ways considered commonplace by an average nineteenth-century European, but also because India was weak and vulnerable, and it *could* be converted to Christianity. The only way Indian people could ward off this invading power was to safeguard their religious faiths from missionary invasion by withdrawing into their *sanctum sanctorum*, which, eventually, resulted in the Hindu religious renaissance, and the founding of the Brahmo Samaj and the Arya Samaj.[32]

Justifying the fear of non-Christian leaders, T.V.Phillip calls

---

30. Quoted in T.V. Philip, "Christianity in Indian During Western Colonial-ism," p. 16
31. Ibid.
32. See R.C. Majumdar, (ed.) *British Paramountcy and Indian Renaissance* (Bombay: Bharatiya Vidya Bhavan, 1965). pp. 97-150.

for an honest re-evaluation of the socio-religio-political situation of nineteenth-century India. He contends that the present India mission history will remain incomplete until it is written against this backdrop of fear and suspicion on the part of non-Christians, aggressive mission activities by the mission societies, and militant administrative policies of the colonizers.[33]

When I attempt to review the colonial mission literature, I do not want to give room for suspicion that colonial mission history as written by European mission societies and Western scholars was nothing more than a fabric of lies, myths, or triumphalistic achievements and that, if the truth about them were to be told, they would simply be blown away. Rather, what I am trying to present is the close-knit strength of colonial mission structure and its intimate ties to the socio-economic, political and cultural institutions that dominated nineteenth-century India.

The Union of Colonialism and Christian Missions

Colonialism and Christian missions went hand-in-hand since the arrival of the Portuguese in India. When the Popes saw the zeal and interest of the Portuguese kings in evangelizing the newly found lands, they entrusted them with the task of converting the natives to Christian faith. Pope Leo X, by his bull *Pro Excellenti* of 1514, and King D. Manuel, the eleventh administrator of *Asia Portuguesa*, with his Vicar-Generals, played important roles in sending missionaries to India.[34]

The vast areas of southern and eastern Asia were placed under Portuguese ecclesiastical jurisdiction, which came to be known as padroado (patronage).[35] According to this system, the Portuguese kings were given power to appoint bishops in any sees created in the newly found regions, and to send missionaries to nurture the converts in Christian faith. The kings also took up the responsibility of making necessary contributions for the

---

33. See T.V. Philip, "Christianity in India During Western Coloniasm," p. 16ff.
34. See George M. Moraes, *A History of Christianity in India (From early times to St. Francis Xavier: A.D. 52-1542)* (Bombay: Manaktalas, 1964), p. 229.
35. See A. Da. Silva Rego, *Historia das Missoes do Padroado Portugues do Oriente India,* Vol. 1 (Lisbon: Agencia Geral Das Conolias, 1949).
36. Joseph Thekkadah, *From the Middle of the Sixteenth to the End of the Seventeenth Century (1542-1700)* (Bangalore: The Church History Association of India, 1982), p.5.

maintenance of the missions and their institutions and for the protection of the neophytes.[36] The role of the Portuguese king in the promotion of missions and the preservation of the converts was very evident when he wrote to D. Francisco de Almeida, the first Portuguese Viceroy to India,

> We recommend that you should favor the Christians in whatever you do, wherever you may find them. You should honor them and have them honoured in everything. In like manner you should also treat the new converts, whatever may be the nationality to which they belong, while both should be catechised and well instructed in the doctrines of the Faith. We wish that you pay special attention to this, because despite the fact that the religious who go (to these countries) do take good care of this, it will be most profitable if you also attend to it. [37]

The kings also began to provide for the evangelization of India and other countries of southern Asia by sending out a number of religious and diocesan priests from Portugal and elsewhere. In exchange, the missionaries were often expected to lead the armies in war times "with the crucifix held high in their hands."[38] This kind of arrangement continued until the arrival of the British and Dutch in India. When the Portuguese were not able to support the missions any longer, Rome created a missionary office known as *Congregatio de Propaganda Fide* (popularly known as the Propaganda) and began to send its own missionaries. This created conflicts between *Padroada and Propaganda Fide*.[39]

The Jesuits, who began their work in 1542, began to grow and by 1584 there were 349 in the Indian Province.[40] As the number began to increase, the Province was divided into North and South: the North with its headquarters at Goa, and the South at Cochin. It was in north India that mission and colonialism went hand-in-hand, conspicuously so from the time of Afonso d' Albuquerque in 1510. He knew full well that, with the meager power Portuguese were wielding in India it would become

---

37. Quoted in George M. Moraes, *A History of Christianity in India,* p. 133.
38. Ibid. p. 241.
39. Ibid. p. 6.
40. Ibid.

impossible to manage the extensive maritime empire which he was planning to establish.

If this empire was to survive, it was imperative that the strategic positions be placed in the hands of trustworthy people. Unlike the Nair women in South India who preferred to marry only Brahmins, the women of Goa were beginning to take an increasing liking to the Portuguese. Albuquerque, therefore, conceived a great plan of rearing a population of half-breeds by encouraging (in some cases forcing) his soldiers and traders to marry these women, after converting them to Christianity. He gave the newly married couples a dowry of 18,000 reas from the state treasury to help them get settled. He was also convinced that if the natives were converted to Christianity they would be loyal to the Portuguese.[41] By 1540 there were 1800 such Portuguese settlers in Goa alone.[42]

The soldiers had also taken a number of concubines and the number began to grow. The intense drive for conversion to Christianity started when the Jesuit missionaries persuaded Governor Barreto to pass laws that would favor Christians and force non-Christians to become Christians. The governor finally yielded and decreed

1) that all the government offices held by the Hindus be taken away from them and be given to the Christians; 2) that Christian converts not be deprived of the right to inherit their share of the family property; 3) that Hindu orphans below the age of reason who had neither parents . . . be brought up in St.Paul's college until they were able to choose their religion for themselves,; 4) that Hindus not be allowed to hold their rites and ceremonies publicly. The governor ordered that these laws should be faithfully observed under pain of severe penalties.[43]

As a result of this ordinance, Goa became almost a Christian territory in 1563 with a Christian population of about 70,000. The Christian population began to grow rapidly, and by the beginning of the seventeenth century, the Hindus became a

---

41. Ibid., p. 311.
42. Ibid.
43. Ibid., p. 317.

minority group in Goa. There were only about 20,000 Hindus while the total population was about 150,000.[44]

Even the outstanding missionaries expected the colonizers to get involved in the missionary work of converting the natives. For example, Francis Xavier, in his letter to the King of Portugal, insisted that the task of converting India to Christ should be taken out of the hands of the missionaries and put into the hands of the civil authorities. He wrote, "But as long as Viceroys are not urged by the fear of disgrace and fine to make many Christians, Your Majesty must not hope that the preaching of the Gospel will meet with great success in India." [45]

As for the southern province, the combined forces of the missionaries and the Portuguese with "enticement and force" helped to successfully to latinize the rite and discipline of the Thomas Christians and brought them under the patronage of the king of Portugal in 1599. In order to extricate themselves from the hands of the Jesuits, the Thomas Christians made several attempts to establish contact with the patriarch in Syria.[46] They were repeatedly obstructed by the Portuguese, which eventually brought about the general revolt of 1653, known as the "Coonan Cross Oath". Since then, the united community has been divided, with about two-thirds following Latin rites and a third re-establishing connection with the Syrian Orthodox church. [47]

In some sense the Portuguese set a precedent for the British in India by combining both mission and State. The impact of their mission lodged in the memory of the natives too long, until the British came. Speaking of the Portuguese power and the Jesuit mission, Sisir Kumar Das has slightly exaggerated but forceful words to say

> The stories of Portuguese savagery haunted the memory of the Bengalis for several centuries and in our own times the novelists exploited these themes with much power and feeling. The conversion of Bengalis into Christianity not only coincided

---

44. Ibid., p. 316.
45. Quoted in T.V. Philip, "Christianity in India During Western Colonialism," p.17.
46. See Thekkadah, *From the Middle of the Sixteenth to the End of the Seventeenth Century,* pp.94-96.
47. The Syrian Orthodox Christians are also known as Jacobites, and *Puthenkur* (the new party). Ibid., pp.91-109.

with the activities of the Portuguese pirates in Bengal, but the pirates took an active interest in it. The Bengalis who accepted Christianity were forced to abandon their faith at the point of sword or they were allured by money.[48]

In spite of all these efforts, the Church did not make any inroads in winning caste Hindus and Muslims in the sixteenth century. There was hardly any encounter between Christianity and Indian culture. The efforts of the Portuguese were mainly confined to small pockets in India where they held political power. Christianity spread mainly among the employees of the Portuguese, Eurasians, and the depressed caste people who lived the southwest coast. Disappointingly, the converts' understanding of Christian faith was too shallow, their moral and ethical character too frivolous, and their life-style failed to serve as an impetus for the surrounding non-Christian masses to emulate.

The first Protestant missionaries to arrive on Indian soil were the two German missionaries, Ziegenbalg and Plutschau, sent by the king of Denmark. They landed in Tranquebar in 1706, a Danish trade post in South India, with a charter from King Frederick IV of Denmark. Since the Danish trade post never crossed the boundary of the Tamil kingdom, their missionary work was confined mainly to the Tamils. The Protestant missionary work gained momentum only after the arrival and the expansion of the Anglican power.[49]

The English East India Company, started as a trade company, began to expand until it became the largest colonial power in history. The Company openly encouraged missionary work until the middle of the eighteenth century. But towards the end of the century, with the annexation of territories and the assumption of administrative responsibilities over Indian territories, the Company decided not to interfere with the traditional cultures of the people by supporting missionary work. This policy of withdrawing support for missionary work did not last too long. After the Company's charters were renewed in 1813 and finally

---

48. Quoted in T.V. Philip, "Christianity in India During Western Colonialism," p. 17.
49. See Arthur Mayhew, *Christianity and the Government of India* (London: Faber & Gwyer Limited, [1931].

in 1833, the Board of Directors changed the policy of the Company and, under pressure from Evangelicals in England the missionaries began to arrive freely in India. Ever since, there has existed a renewed cooperation between the missionaries and the colonial power in helping one another in their missions.[50]

Since I am going to discuss the relationship between the missionaries and the British power in the next two chapters, I am not going to elaborate much of this suzerainty relationship in this section. As I refer to a great deal of written material related to British colonial policy, political doctrine and its commercial setting in my argument, my usage of the word "colonialism" should be defined in this section.

Colonization and Colonialism Explained

The terms colonization and colonialism are synonymously used by scholars who argue that both terms mean the same.[51] Colonization takes the form of political expression of one nation dominating a geographically external political unit inhabited by people of another race and culture with all its attendant evils for material benefits. The term colonialism, on the other hand, represents "an imperialist policy of exploiting colonies to the profit of the mother country alone."[52]

In general usage, these terms are variously defined as the denial of native population 'rights' and the imposition of foreign commercial and political control on a people without their consent. The control of a native population by an alien national or racial group could be achieved without resorting to large-scale human settlement (for example, the "first" British empire in North America or the colonization of Australia) or even without formal territorial rule. In global panorama, one country can control another with mere unilateral economic policies or political philosophies. In my writing colonialism refers to cessation of legal sovereignty or usurping of another national territory by an alien racial group. By the usage "colonial monetrism" I refer to the monetary benefits

---

50. See Eric Stokes, *The English Utilitarians and India* (Oxford: Clarendon Press, 1959).
51. Robert Strausz-Hupe and Harry W. Hazard, eds. *The Idea of Colonialism* (New York: Frederick A. Praeger, Inc, 1958), pp. 17ff.
52. Robert Delavignette, *Christianity and Colonialism*, tr. by J.R. Foster (New York: Hawthorn Books, 1964), p.9.

derived out of the imposition of an alien power and the dominance of the political will of a particular group of people over another for personal gain. Colonial monetrism can be derived either through direct control of power over the natives or through indirect means of controlling the local economy with imperialist business enterprises or legal systems.

The Indian attitude toward colonialism was summarized by Deshbandhu Das in his undelivered presidential address at the Indian National Congress in 1920.

> The cultural conquest of India is all but complete; it was the inevitable result of her political conquest. India must resist it. . . (I hear my moderate friends say:) "why not work out your destiny within the British Empire? My answer is: so long as India occupies the position of a dependent in the British Empire, so long the task cannot be undertaken. . . Economically, the British rule has had a disastrous effect on our national well-being. . . Morally, we are becoming a nation of slaves . . . Intellectually we have become willing victims to the imposition of foreign culture upon us . . . I object then to the perpetuation of British domination . . . that rule may be good or bad – but my conclusion is based on the view that there is inherent in subjection something which injures national life and hampers its growth and fulfillment."[53]

Colonialism was understood as alien invasion, domination, and economic exploitation, and so it must be resisted. This idea of resistance was derived not only from cultural values but also from the scriptural understanding of the Hindu Vedas. Kautilya who wrote *Arthasastra* in the fourth century B.C., condemned foreign rule as an unmitigated evil, the worst form of exploitation *(Vairajya)*. He pointed out that the conqueror subdues a country by violence *(parasyachchidya)* and exploits people by over-taxation and thus drains it of its wealth.[54] Kautilya had seen the conquest of Alexander and tried to liberate the nation from the Greeks.

---

53. *Young India*, January 11, 1922. Also see *Congress Presidential Address*, (Madras, 1934), pp. 538-39.
54. *Kautilya's Arthasastra*, trans. R. Shamasastry (Mysore: Sri Raghuveer Press, 1951).

India's historical landscape is strewn with the wreckage of foreign powers that invaded and conquered it repeatedly to establish their empires. However, no power had affected the Indian people, culture, and nation as a whole as much as the British power did. Greek imperialism, Mogul invasion, Portuguese domination, and their effects were not felt equally by all the Indian people living in the subcontinent. But the British conquest deeply altered Indian society and transformed it to the core.

In the first half of the nineteenth century, Britain dominated the global economy by its industrialization and maritime naval power. Its Companies in the East provided outlets for manufactured goods and sustained a constant supply of raw materials. Soon, Britain realized that her position as a global economic power was challenged by rival European countries and disruptive political and rebellious forces in colonies. After the abolition of slave trade in 1807, Britain was forced to develop her control of India because of its strategic location for trading activity in Asia and because of the advantages of holding onto the Indian army in order to safeguard British interests throughout the East. The Indian military was used to quell insurrection not only within India but also in other colonies in the Far East, the Middle East, and Africa where British interests were threatened. The use of the Indian army to bolster Britain's political and economic interests continued until the end of World War II. India, as a result, became a priceless colony for the British empire.

At the end of the nineteenth century, it appeared as though India had gone under for ever. Its traditional weaving industry had been long since destroyed to make way for Lancashire cotton mills. English education, administration, railways, and modern communication displaced the national culture. The will-power and self-respect of the natives were destroyed and it seemed as though there was no escape from this burden for the colonized. This radical transformation was summarized by Peter Worsely in his book *The Third World.*

Millions of men were driven off the land, some to be turned into plantation—or city-workers, some into semi-unemployed or unemployed 'lumpenproletarians', others to become bandits. Men of high status were cast down; clerks and teachers given new dignitaries. Indigenous commerce struggled against powerful foreign competition, usually backed by a well-disposed government. And the conquered all wore the 'uniform of colour,' not as some external symbol of domination, like the pig-tail forced upon the Chinese by the Manchu, but as part of the flesh of their body.[55]

Through this kind of radical, social metamorphosis which levelled and reduced the people to a pattern, Britain, with its technological superiority and administrative ability, attempted to bring about a radical change in India.

Let me pause here to mention the Muslim reaction to British colonialism. Up until 1920 Muslims in India believed that British rule was a blessing and an equalizer against Hindu dominance; and hence, they hesitated to openly join Hindu leaders in resisting British power. Although the Mutiny of 1857 was considered by British administrators as the work of Muslims against British, Indian scholars such as Majumdar and his associates discount that view. Muslims joined Hindus in the struggle against British power only after the sultan of Turkey, the caliph of Islam, was deposed and his territories dispossessed by British. The association with the Hindus resulted in the establishment of the Khilafat Movement (Caliphate Movement). In the political history of India, the Khilafat Movement was the only movement in which the Muslims and the Hindus collaborated absolutely for a common cause.

The colonial experience endured by Indian people under the British was much different from what the Arabs experienced under the Turks, the Tibetans under the Chinese, the Koreans under the Japanese and the East Europeans under the Russians. Unlike the other overlords, the British categorized the people of its colonies under certain typologies and subjected them to a process of certain simplification. The division of East and West was categorically defined, and the terms "barbarous", "savages", "pagan," and "superstitious" were given to the colonized; the people, the country, and its resources were parcelled out under the name of administration. By the end of the nineteenth century, the doctrine of the newly formulated theory of European superiority

---

55. Peter Worsley, *The Third World* (Chicago: The University of Chicago Press, 1964), p.17.

was preached and practiced. The once respected and diverse cultures of India had been reduced to a common inferiority.[56]

The word "colonialism" as used in this book is not just a generic term meaning alienation and domination. The expression stands for the oppressive rule of the British psychologically, economically, and culturally over the Indians. For example, the British colonizers who used violence to come to power in India introduced numerous kinds of legal systems to end violence, fearing it might subvert their power.

The country which governed its farmer-settler society with its own cultural law was suddenly imposed upon by alien laws, by a foreign government based outside its territory. Indian people were forced to obey a law of which they had no previous knowledge. When the native people were oppressed by British soldiers, traders, plantation owners, or administrators, there was no face-to-face confrontation. The oppressors had to be challenged with superior knowledge of law, enormous sums of money, and administrative skills in courts presided over by European judges. Besides, the Europeans were tried in separate courts under separate law.

When the Indian people had grievances against their overlords, there was no manager to mediate and no ambassador to represent them. The natives were paralyzed and forcefully contained within a structure designed by European colonizers to facilitate their commercial enterprise. That was the most explosive of all types of colonial violence. And this type of violence was perpetuated by the soldiers, traders, administrators, and even missionaries.

---

56. Ibid., p. 26.

CHAPTER III

Theoretical Reason to Study Encounter of Cultures

Colonial mission depended for its strategy on the positional superiority of the missionaries, which put them in a series of possible relationship with the natives. Their close ties with the expansionists and colonial imperialists gave them a steady source of income to carry on the mission.[57] In fact, missionaries were able to carry on their work in India with the help of colonial monetrism and European patriotism. One of their main aims in converting the natives was to make them loyal to the British Empire.[58] It is this argument that I expand in subsequent chapters.

In order to substantiate my argument, I have found it extremely useful to employ Michel Foucault's notion of discourse, as explained in *The Archaeology of Knowledge* and in *Discipline and Punish*, and Edward Said's concept of texts as worldly and circumstantial, as described in *The World, the Text and the Critic* and *Beginnings: Intention and Method*. Without analyzing the colonial mission literatures as a discourse, it is hardly possible to understand the vast body of literature produced by the mission societies.

Nineteenth-century colonial mission policies were not produced in a vacuum. They were created, fashioned and executed in the British colonial, cultural, socio-economic, and political setting. Mission literature was produced in these contexts. And since there is an intrinsic "connection between texts and the existential actualities of human life, politics, societies, and events,"[59] the actual realities of power and authorities should also be studied in order to understand the mission texts. Said argues that it is this "connection" that makes texts possible and delivers them to the readers. Therefore, "Texts are worldly, to some degree they are events, and, even when they appear to deny it, they are nevertheless a part of the social world, human life, and of course

---

57. Robert Adler, *Western Missions*, pp. 6ff., 60.
58. Henry Stebbing Sermon, *A Sermon Preached before the Incorporate Society for the Propagation of the Gospal in Foreign Parts*, (London: E. Owen, 1742), p. 78.
59. Edward Said, *World, Text and Critic*, p. 4.

the historical moments in which they are located and interpreted."[60]

Said concludes, therefore, that all texts exist in context. They have political and ideological circumstances. They are enmeshed in circumstance, time, place and society and hence they are worldly.[61] Therefore, it is important to study the culture, power, and hegemonic influence of the colonizers and the missionaries that affected the lives of people in India. What is "worldly and circumstantial" to Said is "contextualization" to Christian theologians, or "circumstantial reality" to Paul Ricouer. In his book, *Orientalism*, Said explains that all the above influences play an important role in the production of literatures and so they must be studied in context.

That politics in the form of imperialism bears upon the production of literature, scholarship, social theory, and history writing is by no means equivalent to saying that culture is therefore a demeaned and denigrated thing . . . we can better understand the persistence and the durability of saturating hegemonic systems like culture when we realize that their internal constraints upon writers and thinkers were productive, not unilaterally inhibiting.[62]

Since the colonial mission literature has both an internal consistency and a highly articulated set of external relationships to the dominant culture surrounding it, we should analyze the mission's shape and internal structure, its pioneers, its reports, its sponsors, its origin and its practice. We should also try to look deeper into the structure of mission in order to study how its literatures borrowed, and were frequently informed by, strong ideas, religious doctrines, and political trends ruling the culture. Hence all of society's activities at a given time (literary, political, religious, and social in the narrower sense of the mores, class, and imperial relations) constitute an organic, ultimately coherent political, cultural, and historical whole.

---

60. Ibid.
61. Edward Said, *Beginnings: Intention and Method* (New York: Basic Books, 1975), pp. 81-88.
62. Edward Said, *Orientialism*, p. 14.

When I employ the word "culture," I refer to the prevailing European culture and its hegemonic influence upon colonized people, its elevated position to dominate, to rule, to differentiate and decide what is good or bad for them. This usage is similar to that employed by Raymond Schwab, Michel Foucault, and Edward Said.[63]

Cultural change comes about not so much from the experience of groups of people in a given society but from culture-producing organizations such as colonialism, English education, Western religion and so on. This notion has been deemphasized in history and mission literature. Concurring with this concept, Talcott Parsons describes cultural change as a process of "value generalization" issued by the growing complexity of social patterns. He writes, "When the network of socially structured situations becomes more complex, the value pattern itself must be couched at a higher level of generality in order to ensure social stability."[64] Parsons cites examples of changes in religious conceptions, legal codes, and theoretical knowledge, and concludes that these constitute the critical form of cultural change. "The generalization of value system can effectively regulate social action without relying upon pluralistic prohibitions. This has been a central factor in the modernization process."[65] The act of imposing a generalization of value patterns was done in stages by the British.

The modernization adopted by the colonizers (which I explain elaborately in the next chapter) through the introduction of Western jurisprudence, commercial regulations, religious restrictions, taxation, English education, and so on, altered the social life of the colonized Indian people. Pseudo-modernization introduced in the nineteenth century not only led to an uprooting of rural and urban communities but also to a potential disorientation. As a result, the aliens could rule the natives with simple but strong legal and political ideologies.

---

63. See Raymond Schwab, *The Orientation Renaissance: Europe's Rediscovery of India and the East, 1680-1880,* trans. by Gene Patterson—Black and Victor Reinking (New York: Columbia University Press, 1984), Michel Foucault, *The Archaeology of Knowledge,* Edward Said, *Beginnings: Intention and Method.*

64. Talcott Parsons, *Societies: Evolutionary and Comparative Persepctives,* (Englewood Cliffs, N.J.: Prentice Hall, 1971), p. 27.

65. Ibid., p. 15.

All ideologies, says Robert Wuthnow in *Communities of Discourse*, grow under the careful cultivation of particular movements which arise in specific places and bear specific relations to their surroundings. For instance, Wuthnow argues that the Reformation grew in well-organized urban areas, well-structured secular and ecclesiastical hierarchies, and within well-educated ranks of the clergy. The Enlightenment thrived in salons, academies, bureaus, and universities. The Socialist movement flourished in party offices, legislative halls, and clandestine associations. "Broadly speaking, institutional contexts are the organizational positions and relations that form the matrix in which ideas are produced and disseminated, including the relations between these organizations and other institutions in the broader environment."[66] Therefore, Wuthnow insists that the interplay of the leaders of powerful ruling institutions and the powerless receiving audiences of common origin should be analyzed in order to understand the origin and production of ideologies.

Colonial culture and its ideologies were imposed upon India by a dominant class of administrators and bureaucrats from England. At the height of power and privilege they were determined to disseminate European political principles and expand British colonial institutions by governing from above. This downward movement of culture from above penetrated into the powerless society, as Matthew Arnold argues, through great men of prevailing culture and State able to contend forcefully with the existing ideologies, philosophies, values, and beliefs. This penetrative cultural movement assertively instills an identifiable set of beliefs and ideas upon the society.[67]

Thus the power of culture which percolates from above, Said argues, becomes potentially nothing less than the power of State.

---

66. Robert Wuthnow, *Communities of Discourse* (Cambridge, Massachusetts: Harvard University Press, 1989), p. 546.

67. "The great men of culture are those who have had a passion for diffusing, for making prevail, for carrying from one end of society to the other, the best knowledge, the best ideas of the time; who have laboured to divest knowledge of all that was harsh, uncouth, difficult, abstract, professional, exclusive; to humanize it, to make it efficient outside the clique of the cultivated and learned, yet still remaining the best knowledge and thought of the time and a true source, of sweetness and light" as written by Matthew Arnold in *Culture and Anarchy*, ed. J.Dover Wilson (Cambridge: Cambridge University Press, 1969), p. 70.

To be in and for a culture is to be in and for a State in a compelling loyal way. With this assimilation of culture to the authority and exterior frame work of the State go as well such things as assurance, confidence, the majority sense, the entire matrix of meanings we associate with "home," belonging and community. Outside this range of meanings . . . stand anarchy, culturally disenfranchised, those elements opposed to culture and State: the homeless, in short.[68]

And while commenting on Arnold's concluding remarks on the intertwining of culture and State Said asserts

This means that culture is a system of discrimination and evaluation . . . for a particular class in the State able to identify with it; it also means that culture is a system of exclusion legislated from above but enacted through its polity, by which such things as anarchy, disorder, irrationality, inferiority, bad taste, and immorality are identified, then deposited outside the culture and kept there by the power of the State and its institutions.[69]

And so it can be argued that it is the prevailing culture's social and economic barometer that determines what is good and appropriate for people and what is not; what is to be retained in a society and what is to be discarded. How this cultural norm is used as an institutionalized process to consider what is appropriate to be retained, encouraged and used, and what is to be eliminated has been demonstrated by Foucault in *Madness and Civilization, The Order of Things, The History of Sexuality,* and *Discipline and Punish.*[70] It was on this scale that Indian culture was weighed by the colonizers and missionaries and found wanting. That was why, as a first measure, Thomas Babington Macaulay introduced

---

68. Edward Said, *World, Text and Critic,* p.11.
69. Ibid.
70. Michel Foucault *Madness and Civilization: A History of Insanity in the age of Reason* trans. R. Howard (New York: Vintage/Random House, 1973); *The Order of Things: An Archaeology of Human Science* (New York: Vintage/Random House, 1973); *The History of Sexuality* trans. Robert Hurley, (New York: Vintage/Random House, 1980); *Discipline and Punish: The British of the Prison,* trans. Alan Sheridan, (New York: Vintage/Random House, 1979).

English education in India, to educate and civilize the Indians and eventually to develop European tastes so they would buy English manufactured goods.[71]

Macaulay had calculated with confidence that Western science would remove all traces of idolatry in India in forty years.[72] He believed, with his brother-in-law Charles Trevelyan, "that large and continuous doses of western knowledge would not only purge [India] of Hindu and Islamic religion, but also build up a new India with an essentially Christian constitution."[73]

However, missionaries were afraid that the mere introduction of Western education, science, and philosophy would make the Indians atheists or agnostics. Hence they asked for the introduction of the Bible in the academic curriculum. Between 1829-57 legal and social reforms were introduced to protect Christianity and its converts. Alexander Duff and John Wilson in close association with Macaulay and Charles Trevelyan and "other devotees of 'useful information' and 'western sciences' felt behind them the moral support of Bourgham and John Stuart Mill" and they succeeded in achieving their goal.[74]

Duff and Wilson tried to persuade the government and mission societies to grant funds to mission schools and introduce religious instruction. Arthur Mayhew summarizes the efforts of Duff and Wilson and says, "It was Duff who . . . convinced the Mission world by the success of his experiments and the persistent fearlessness of his speeches and pamphlets, that success depended on the enlightenment of India by Christian secondary school and colleges."[75]

Both the Evangelicals and liberals in Europe believed that the introduction of European knowledge and civilization was the panacea for all social evil in India and this would disrupt Indian social tradition to make them embrace Christianity. "The conversion of India would thus be accomplished without resort to coercive power of the state."[76] This pride in European knowledge

71. Thomas Babington Macaulay *Complete Works*, vol. 11 (London: Longman, 1866), pp. 583-84.

72.. See Charles E. Trevelyan *Life and Letters of Lord Macaulay*, vol. 1 (New York, 1871), pp. 77-98.

73. Arthur Mayhew *Christianity and the Governmenment of India*, pp. 165-166.

74. Ibid., p. 111.

75. Ibid., p. 131.

76. Charles E. Trevelyan *On the Education of the People of India* (London:

and religion was well reflected when Macaulay compared the
European collection of literatures with Indians.

I have no knowledge of either Sanskrit or Arabic. But I have
done what I could to form a correct estimate of their value. I
have read translations of the most celebrated Arabic and
Sanskrit works. I have conversed, both here and at home,
with men distinguished by their proficiency in the Eastern
tongues. I am quite ready to take the oriental learning at the
valuation of the orientalist themselves. I have never found
one among them who could deny that a single shelf of a good
European library was worth the whole native literature of
India and Arabia. The intrinsic superiority of the Western
literature is indeed fully admitted by those members of the
committee who support the oriental plan of education . . . It
is, I believe, no exaggeration to say that all the historical
information which has been collected in the Sanskrit language
is less valuable than what may be found in the paltry
abridgements used at preparatory schools in England. In every
branch of physical or moral philosophy, the relative position
of the two nations is nearly the same.[77]

Macaulay's statement had a far-reaching effect upon the people
of India. He was one of Matthew Arnold's men of prevailing
culture and, speaking from a position of power and authority, he
could translate his opinion into governmental legislation so as to
make an entire subcontinent of people study in a language not
their own.

In fact Macaulay helped implement English education in India
on 7 March 1835. Within twenty years the subcontinent
experienced a proliferation of English medium schools and colleges,
mostly run by missionaries. A conservative estimate would give
a total of 180 English institutions and 30,000 students in attendance
in 1854.[78] And six years after the opening of the universities,
English historical and philosophical works penetrated every corner

---

Longmans, 1838), p. 185.
77 Quoted T. Philip D. Curtin, ed., *Imperialism* (New York: Walker and Company, 1971), p. 175.
78. Bruce T. McCully, *English Education and the Origins of Indian Nationalism* (Gloucester, Mass: Peter Smith, 1966), p. 129.

of British India.[79] In Bombay and Madras Presidencies "English education on the *downward-filtration* (italics mine) plan was the accepted order of the day."[80]

When the idea of Western education was successfully implemented by the end of the century, Sir Charles Trevelyan chuckled and wrote,

> The period of dissension and controversy has passed, and the period of action has arrived. In this respect the subject of native education is at the same stage as most of the other great questions relating to India. Hitherto we have been occupied in founding our denomination in India; and in acquiring our experience, but now we have served our novitiate: we know in every point what is required for the benefit of India to make it a great and flourishing country; and the time for giving effect to this knowledge has arrived.[81]

What we see here is the confident proclamation of a powerful man making assertive claim about the future destiny of millions of politically imprisoned and economically incarcerated people. A handful of mighty colonial administrators have determined to shape the course of the hostage colonized country as they deem good for their subjugated victims.

As a result, the dialectics of Hindu philosophy and the subtleties of Islamic law disappeared from curriculum.[82] This is just one example of a powerful man deciding what is good for millions of people of another country who supposedly did not measure up to the standards of the European culture, religion and civilization. Through this kind of aggressive policy, men of "prevailing culture" attempted to unite two cultures and the civilizations of people without common bonds, tongue, sentiment, thought, aspirations, culture, or values and with opposing views of human life and religious faith.

---

79. George O. Trevelyan *The Competition Wallah*, 2nd ed. (London, 1866), pp. 330-331.
80. Ibid., p. 130.
81. Charles E. Trevelyan, *Parliamentary Papers, 1852-53* (London: G.E. Eyre & W. Spottiswoode, 1855).
82. *Report of the Indian Education Commission appointed by the Resolution of the Government of India, 3rd February, 1882* (Calcutta, 1883).

This union of British expansionism, trusteeship and sense of superiority can also be seen in the writings of Sir Standford Raffles.[83] The following references may help us understand the superior attitude of British administrators and their high-handed policy in dealing with the people for personal, material gain. After depicting the enormous profit Britain would gain by improving the plight of the people and the economic condition of India, David Laurie concluded by observing

> This comprises no presumptuous view of our character; it is Britain that now gives to the world the standard of all that is excellent—it is to British manners and customs that all nations now conform themselves—Britain leads the fashion and gives the law, not merely in the tinsel of dress, but in the whole frame of social acquirements.[84]

> It appears to me that there is something in our national character and condition that fits us for this exalted station. I think too, there is a kind of destination of this character and condition to these services. It was the privilege of Britain to receive the first and the purest beams of the reformed religion."[85]

This was also true of missionaries who were involved in mission work. The object of converting people was usually envisaged as a means to some extraneous end. For instance, John Shebbeare wrote that missionaries would be the most powerful persons on earth to unite the nations more strongly to the English interest, for "he who rules the soul, rules everything."[86]

The customary position of those who planned to take the Gospel to "pagan nations" was summarized in the sermon preached by Henry Stebbing at The Society for the Propagation of the Gospel meeting.

---

83. Sir Reginald Coupland *Raffles* (London: Oxford University Press, 1926).
84. David Laurie *Hints Regarding the East India Monopoly* (Glasgow, R. Chapman Printed for Gale & Curties, 1813), p. 5.
85. Ibid., p. 51.
86. John Shebbeare *Letters on the English Nations,* 2nd ed., (London: S. Crowder, 1756), p. 65.

When some hear of "Propagating Gospel in Foreign Parts" they are apt to think of nothing else, but converting Heathen Nations to the Christian Faith . . . But, whoever, looks into our Charter, will find, that the first and principal End of this Corporation is, not to plant Christianity among Heathens, but, to restore, or to preserve it among Christians . . . The converting of Heathens is a secondary, incidental Point.[87]

Stebbing also thought that civilizing heathens was the prerequisite to conversion.[88] The SPG (1701) was followed by the establishment of the Methodists, the Baptist Missionary Society (1792), the London Missionary Society (1795), the Church Missionary Society (1799), the British and Foreign Bible Society (1804), and the London Society for Promoting Christianity among the Jews (1808). All these mission societies became exceedingly powerful by the middle of the nineteenth century and "openly joined the expansion of Europe."[89] The essence of the missionary movement, argues Moore, was an aggressive cultural imperialism, propaganda for the spread of European ideas and ideals over the face of the globe.[90]

William Wilberforce said that the Indian natives were idolatrous and superstitious with a "feeble knowledge of God," their divinities were "absolute monsters of lust, injustice and wicked," and the people themselves were barbarous and low in the scale of European civilization. Hence they should be civilized and converted.[91] Charles Grant talked about India as Sodom and Gomorrah and said only Western mind and Christian truth will liberate those heathens.[92]

Some secular cultural heroes, such as John Stuart Mill, Matthew Arnold, John Ruskin, Charles Dickens, and George Eliot, also joined British administration in deciding what was good for the natives. John Stuart Mill, for example, made it clear

---

87. Henry Stebbing, *A Sermon Preached Before the Incorporate Society for the Propagation of the Gospel in Foreign Parts,* p. 18.

88. Ibid., p. 19.

89. A.L. Tibawi, *British Interest 1800-1901* (London: Oxford University Press, 1961), p. 5.

90. R.C. Moore, *Spread of Christianity,* p. 19.

91. Speech of William Wilberforce *Hansard,* 22 June, 1813, First Series, Vol 26: p. 164.

92. Charles Grant *Observation,* p. 71.

in his book *On Liberty and Representative Government* that his
views on Europe could not be applied to India because Indian
people were civilizationally inferior.[93] In the third volume of
Dissertation and Discussion, again, Mill spoke of the absence of
rights for barbarians.[94] In the final chapter of *Representative
Government* he argued that India's civilization had "not attained
the requisite degree of development" and so his views about
Europe could not be applied to India.[95]

If we analyze nineteenth-century texts, we find them replete
with similar disparaging remarks. Speaking of this kind of double
standard manifested in European history and literatures, Said
laments

> The entire history of nineteenth-century European thought
> is filled with such discriminations as these, made between
> what is fitting for us and what is fitting for them, the former
> designated as inside, in place, common, belonging, in a word
> *above*, the latter, who are designated as outside, excluded,
> aberrant, inferior, in a word *below* . . . The large cultural-
> national designation of European culture as the privileged
> norm carried with it a formidable battery of other distinctions
> between ours and theirs, between proper and improper,
> European and non-European, higher and lower: they are to
> be found everywhere in such subjects and quasi-subjects as
> linguistics, history, philosophy, anthropology and even biology.[96]

Therefore, it is important to study nineteenth-century mission
history of India from this background and to analyze the text
from post-colonial perspectives. In this respect I would agree
with T.V.Philip when he argues that the study of European mission
history in India "is a study of encounter of cultures [and hence]
. . . [it] is the task of the historian to examine the process and
value of these encounters."[97] Since this encounter reached its

---

93. Eric Stokes, *English Utilitarians and India,* p. 298.
94. See John Stuart Mill, *Dissertations and Discussion: Philosophical and Historical* (Edinburgh: Westminster, 1859).
95. John Stuart Mill, *On Liberty and Representative Government,* 2nd ed. (London: J.M. Parker & Son, 1838).
96. Edward Said, *World, Text and Critic,* p. 14.
97. T.V. Philip, "Christianity in India During Western Colonialism," p. 4.

peak during the British colonial period and several volumes of literature have been produced by European scholars about that time, it is imperative for us to "analyse the extent and the nature of relationship between colonialism and Christian missions."[98]

The Task of a Historian

In his book *The Archaeology of Knowledge* Foucault argues that history is not a unified, linear succession of events; rather it is "a stable structure."[99] History contains inherent "cracks" or "discontinuities." Discontinuity is not an "external condition" to be reduced in the traditional sense. On the other hand, discontinuity plays the role of a "working concept" to measure "the mutations that operate" in the field of history.[100] A historian's job, therefore, is to locate the sites of discontinuities by questioning the documents used in a discourse and the "ideologies and totalizations" which form the context of that discourse.

The historian has to bring out the hidden, suppressed voices of the discourse. In this process the historian has to

Reconstruct another discourse, rediscover the silent murmurings, the inexhaustible speech that animates from within the voice that one hears, reestablish the tiny, invisible text that runs between and sometimes collides with them.[101]

In other words, a historian is to locate and identify the mute, inarticulate voice of the discourse behind the apparently well enunciated, stable surface of discourse.

In *Power and Knowledge* Foucault talks about "buried, subjugated knowledge." Subjugated knowledge, according to Foucault, relates to the historical contents that have been buried and disguised in a functionalist and formal systematization. The reason, in fact, for bringing out the inarticulate voice is that it is a hollow that undermines from within all that is said.[102] An analysis of this "not-said" involves a critical scrutiny of the

---

98. Ibid.
99. Michel Foucault, *Archaeology of Knowledge,* p. 6.
100. Ibid., p. 15.
101. Ibid., p. 27.
102. Michel Foucault, *Power/Knowledge,* pp. 25, 81, 83.

"speaking subjects" and "the institutional sites"; therefore, what is recorded is not a "natural" representation of reality.

The historian's research struggles to find out the relationship between the speaking subjects of the discourse and other social, cultural, and political institutions to which they are related. The historian analyzes the speaking subjects in the network of cultural and political interest and forces.

Foucault, in fact, argues that there is an internal relationship between power and knowledge. Hence he wants historians to question the objective nature of documents.

> We should admit . . . that *power and knowledge* directly imply one another; that there is *no power relation without the correlative constitution of a field of knowledge* that does not presuppose and constitute at the same time power relations. These *power/knowledge* relations are to be analyzed, therefore, not on the basis of a subject of knowledge who is or is not free in relation to the power system, but, on the contrary, the subject who knows, the objects to be known and the modalities of knowledge must be regarded as so many effects of these fundamental implications of power/knowledge and their historical transformations. In short, it is not the activity of the subject of knowledge that produces a corpus of knowledge, useful or resistant to power, but *power/knowledge,* the process and struggle that traverse it and of which it is made up, that determines the forms and possible domains of knowledge.[103] [Emphasis mine.]

Ideological forces play an important role in the formation of a discourse. Hence discourse has to be placed in a larger context of power to correctly understand it.

Seen in the context of power, where the discourse is formed, the knowledge of the speaking subject becomes a privileged one. The persons who are the subject of inquiry or study become subordinate objects. They are introduced, divided, classified and apportioned out in reports. According to Foucault, discursive

---

103. Hubert L. Dreyfus and Paul Rabinow, *Michel Foucault: Beyond Structuralism and Hermeneutics* (Chicago: The University of Chicago Press, 1983), p. 113.

relationships "determine the group of relations that discourse must establish in order to speak of this or that subject, in order to deal with them, classify them, explain them."[104]

Division, contrast, regrouping, and ordering are done by the privileged speaking subjects in the context of a network of cultural and political institutions. The relations between the speaking subjects and established institutions, economic, and social processes do not define the internal coherence of the object. Rather they enable the object to appear, "to be placed in a field of exteriority."[105] In other words, discursive relations provide the object about which they are talking.

My position, therefore, is that nineteenth-century mission history written by European scholars was culturally conditioned, politically one-sided, and missiologically limited. For instance, after the displacement of Muslim nobility, the Muslims in India were regarded as "a race ruined under British rule."[106] The Muslims reached "the lowest depths of broken pride, black despair and general penury."[107] The Christian missionaries, seeing the fall of Muslim hierarchy and the conquest of India by the Company, considered the success a victory of Christianity over Indian religions. For example, after the defeat of Tipu Sultan in the Carnatic War in 1799, James Hugh, a Christian historian, wrote, "It pleased the Lord of Hosts' on that occasion to crown the British arms with success, and to deliver His servants from the perils that encompassed them."[108]

Even after Mutiny 1857, when British supremacy was re-established in India, J.C. Marshman wrote in *The history of India from the Earliest Period to the Close of Lord Dalhousie's Administration* that the British victory was an act of divine providence.[109] Further, Frederick Cooper, a civil servant of the

---

104. Michel Foucault, *Archaeology of Knowledge,* p. 46.
105. Ibid., p. 45.
106. William H. Hunter, *The Indian Musulmans* (Delhi: Indological Book House), p. 144.
107. B.R. Ambedkar, *Thoughts on Pakistan* (Bombay: Thallker & Co., 1941), p. 43.
108. James Hugh, *The History of Christianity in India,* vol. 3 (London: Seeley and Barnside, 1839), p. 335.
109. J.C. Marshman, *The History of India from the Earliest to the Close of Lord Dalhousie's Administration,* 3 vols. (London: Longmans, Green, 1887), vol 2, p. 27.

Punjab, commenting on the victory of the British, mentioned,

> Wisdom and . . . heroism are still but mere dross before the
> manifest and wondrous interposition of Almighty God in the
> cause of Christianity . . . To those fond of reading signs, we
> would point to the solitary golden cross still gleaming aloft
> on the summit of the Christian church in Delhi, whole and
> untouched. . . . The cross symbolically triumphant over a
> shattered globe![110]

Similar sentiment was shared by Robert Montgomery, the
Lieutenant-Governor of the Punjab when he wrote to his
predecessor, John Lawrence, "It was not policy, or soldiers, or
officers, that saved the Indian Empire to England, and saved
England to India. The Lord our God, He it was."[111]

The same views were expressed by European historians as
well. Christian Lessen, the famous Norwegian historian who taught
in the University of Bonn, wrote his monumental *Indische
Alterthumskunde* in the nineteenth century. In his book he applied
Hegelian dialectic philosophy to the Indian religions and general
history. According to him, the Hindu period of Indian history
was the thesis, the Muslim period the antithesis (negative Prinzip)
and the British Raj the synthesis. This synthesis, to Lessen, in
the form of Christian supremacy was the direct outcome of Indian
history. He wrote, "[In] the world of religion and thought,
Christianity unites and transmutes all that is of value in Hinduism
and Islam."[112]

As a result, European historians and free thinkers began to
propose that backward India should be modernized and
Christianized on the European model. C.H.Philips observed that
after conquering India, the British found a land "resembling in
some respects their own idea of the Europe of middle ages, or
even of the ancient empires described by Herodotus," and wondered
whether to modernize or preserve its institution and govern

---

110. Quoted in Edward Thompson, *The Other Side of the Medal*, (New York:
Harcourt, Brace and Company, 1928), p. 46.
111. Ibid., p. 66.
112. Quoted by A.L. Basham, "Modern Historians of Anceint India," in C.H.
Philips, ed., *Historians of India, Pakistan, and Ceylon* (London: Oxford University Press, 1961), p. 265.

them.[113] But Charles Grant went farther than others and wrote in *Observation* that only Western religion and learning could transform India as "the fabric of Indian social life has been so corrupted by a false religion."[114] With his strong faith in the superiority of Christianity, he urged the Company Directors to open its territories for missionary work.

However, the most influential person who shaped public opinion in Europe in the beginning of the nineteenth century was James Mill. His books, particularly *History of British India*, became text books at Haileybury College in England (the sister college of Fort William College of Calcutta) where the Company's Civil Servants were trained from 1809 to 1855. He was prompted by his friend and master, Jeremy Bentham.[115] He found nothing useful in India; only European civilization could redeem it.

In 1867, J.C.Marshman wrote three volumes of *The History of India*. He too saw "a mysterious but inexorable necessity" that had caused the British presence in India. He wrote, "A Company of merchants in London thus became the instrument, under the mysterious, but wise and benignant agency of Divine Providence, of establishing the British empire in India."[116]

The British always considered opposition to their rule to have religious origins. They felt Islam to be the real source of danger to British authority. Warning his country men, William Hunter wrote, "If India becomes Mohammedan, it may develop an energy which, though temporary, may be lost for centuries . . . it may rise to great heights of a certain kind of Oriental Civilization."[117] To "prevent this conversion of an empire to a false and entirely non-progressive creed," Hunter suggested, the force of Christianity be used.[118]

The most influential book written in the middle of the nineteenth century justifying the intermingling of mission and

113. C.H. Phillips, *Historians of India,* p. 217.
114. Ainslie T. Embree, *Charles Grant and British Rule in India* (New York: Columbia University Press, 1962), pp. 9, 10.
115. James Mill, *The History of British India,* 3 vols. (London: Baldwin, Cardock, and Jay, 1820).
116. J.C. Marshman, *The History of India,* vol. 2, p. 27.
117. William Hunter, "Islam and Christianity in India," *The Contemporary Review,* No. clvix, vol. LII (Feb. 1888), p. 170.
118. Ibid., p. 171.

administration was *The Life of Mahomet from Oriental Sources*
by Sir William Muir, the Lieutenant-Governor of North-Western
Province. He wrote this book at the request of a missionary,
Pfander. Muir's goal was to prove that Indian religions, particularly
Islam, were evil in origin and Christianity was the truly divine
representation. In his book Muir tried to justify the programs of
the colonial government and mission work. Commenting on the
purpose of the book, Norman Daniel said that Muir attempted to
bring "together three different worlds: that of scholarship, that
of government, and that of mission."[119]

As a first measure, in the middle of the nineteenth century,
the British government and missionaries worked together in
introducing the European model of education in India. They hoped
and believed that English education would civilize and Christianize
the Indian people; or, as Macaulay said, such an attempt would
produce a people brown in color but European in taste.

The following chapters demonstrate how nineteenth-century
mission history has been written from the colonizers' point of
view. The historians' philosophy was built on the premise of
India as the other. Christian mission and European colonial
administration shared a common vision of civilizing and
Christianizing the people in India. Moore was not far from truth
when he said that the colonial missionary movement was part of
European cultural propaganda for the spread of European ideologies
over the face of the globe.[120]

---

119. Norman Daniel, *Islam, Europe and Empire* (Edinburgh: The University
Press, 1966), p. 279.
120. R.C. Moore, *The Spread of Christianity*, p. 19.

CHAPTER IV

The Evangelicals and the East India Company

The East India Company was a commercial organization. Its primary motive was trade and profits. Although it paid lip-service to missionary work, never did it take keen interest in the conversion of the people, nor did it encourage the missionaries to do any kind of evangelistic work.[121] After the fall of the Moguls in India, the British became more committed to their permanent establishment of trade in India and conquered Bengal in 1757, which eventually became the nerve center of their political, commercial and intellectual developments in India. Although the Act of 1698 ordered the Company's chaplains to "instruct the Gentoos"[122] in the Protestant faith apart from their duties as chaplains to the Company servants, the Company took no interest in it, fearing that the introduction of an alien religion would excite the already religiously torn country and that the empire would be brought to ruin. As a result, the Directors of the Company got a resolution passed in England that any adventurer or missionary should receive the license of the Company to enter India. An unlicensed adventurer or missionary was liable, on discovery, to expulsion from the Company's territories.[123] This insulated the Company from commercial interlopers who were considered a threat to the trade monopoly and from missionaries who were regarded as a threat to the religiously sensitive Indian public.[124]

In 1793 Charles Grant and other evangelicals in England tried to secure the inclusion of a clause in the Company's Charter requiring the Company to let missionaries work in India. But the Court of Directors of the Company, with the help of their supporters, strongly opposed the demands of the evangelicals

---

121. Kenneth Scott Latourette, *A History of the Expansion of Christianity*, vol. 3, p. 277.

122. Stephen Charles Neill, *The Story of the Christian Church in India and Pakistan* (Grand Rapids, Mi: Wm. B. Erdmans Publishing Co., 1970), p. 51.

123. Ibid., p. 64.

124. P. J. Marshall, *Problems of Empire: Britian and India 1757-1813* (London: George Allen & Unwin Ltd., 1968), pp. 71-72.

and secured their defeat.[125] Defying the policy of the Company, the same year William Carey of the Baptist Missionary Society arrived in Bengal.[126]

Published travel logs and stories about people living in other parts of the world generated interest among people in Britain. Captain James Cook's published accounts of his three voyages to the South Seas between 1768 and 1780 engendered enthusiasm among young people [such as William Carey of the Baptist Missionary Society and Thomas Haweis of the London Missionary Society] and challenged them to go as missionaries to those countries. Brian Stanley, in his book *The Bible and the Flag*, summarizes the general mood of the last decades of the eighteenth century.

> British horizons in the second half of the eighteenth century were dominated by the East India Company rule in India. By the end of the century, 'Asia', which to most English men in the seventeenth century had retained its biblical location in the Near East, had become almost a synonym for India. Indian affairs were the subject of extended parliamentary enquiry and public debate in 1767, 1772-73, 1781-83, and supremely during the trial of Warren Hastings from 1787 to 1795. The demands in Parliament by Edmund Burke and others that British power in India should be exercised in a moral function for the benefit of the native population, found their Christian reflection in the plans of Evangelicals such as Charles Grant, David Brown and Claudius Buchanan for missionary work in India.[127]

In spite of the exclusion policy of the Company, a limited but increasing number of British missionaries came to India during the period between 1793 and 1813. Some were there because two influential members of the Court of Directors, Charles Grant

---

125. Ernest Marshall Howse, *Saints in Politics* (Toronto: University of Toronto Press, 1952), pp. 71-72.

126. E. Daniel Potts, "The Baptist Missionaies of Serampore and the Government of India, 1792-1813, "*Journal of Ecclesiastical History* (March 1964), pp. 229-246.

127. Brian Stanley, *The Bible and the Flag*, (Leicester LEI 7GB: Appolos, IVF), p. 58.

and Edward Parry, were very sympathetic to the christianizing of India and used their power to send out as Company Chaplains evangelicals such as Henry Martyn and Claudius Buchanan, who served both as preachers to the Europeans and as missionaries to the Indians.[128] Other missionaries were members of the Baptist Missionary Society and London Missionary Society, and had literally sneaked into India to take up their station, depending upon the good will of the local officials of the Company to allow them to remain. They were always ready to fall back upon the hospitality of the Danes at Serampore and Tranquebar and the Dutch at Chinsurah.

Twenty years later, when the Charter was to be renewed in 1833, the Parliament debated again the issue of the religion and morals of the people in India. In the meantime, the evangelicals were rallying for the access of Christian missionaries to the Company's dominions. Their ceaseless effort to create a sense of obligation to the natives in India by sending out missionaries and teachers began to gain momentum. Charles Grant, in alliance with William Wilberforce, Zachary Macaulay, Thornton, Henry Venn, and their newly organized body of evangelicals known as the Clapham Sect,[129] began to mobilize public opinion in order to secure free entry for missionaries to India, which had failed in 1795. The two major items on their agenda were the abolition of the Slave Trade and freedom for the mission societies to send missionaries to India. The plan adopted by them was to stir their countrymen's sense of moral duty to the empire and to convince them of India's need for the Gospel.

This theme was elaborately developed in Grant's *Observation on the State of Society among the Asiatic Subjects of Great Britain, etc.*, which Wilberforce caused to be printed and widely distributed. The task of the evangelicals in opening the East Indian colonies for missionary presence was further facilitated by the growing demand of the free traders. When the Company's charter came for renewal before the Parliament in 1813, the evangelicals received the most willing support.[130] As a result, the Charter Act of 1813,

---

128. C.H. Philips, *The East India Company* (Manchester: Manchester University Press, 1961), pp. 159ff.

129. See Ernest Marshall Howse, *Saints in Politics: The Clapham Sect and the Growth of Freedom* (London: Allen & Unwin, 1952).

130. A.T. Embree, *Charles Grant and British Rule in India*, pp. 274-275.

besides creating an Indian Episcopal See, facilitated the entry of missionaries into India and provided that the Government of India would spend up to 10,000 pounds Sterling a year on education from its surplus revenues, if any.[131]

In the meantime, by 1813 Wellesley's conquest of Indian territories produced a debt burden for the Company. The Company lost its Indian trade monopoly in 1813 and could not sell its goods in England as much as previously. As a result, the Company experienced a severe loss of revenue and became a mere military and administrative agency. In order to revive its economic success and finance tea trade with China, the Company resorted to a monopoly over opium trade.

By 1833, the year the Company put an end to all restrictions upon the entry of missionaries, Carey died. However, one significant change which occurred in Bengal was the proliferation of mission societies in and around the Calcutta area. Of the seventy-one stations belonging to various missionary societies working in Bengal, thirty were situated in and around Calcutta, the political nerve-center of the British colonizers.[132]

The evangelicals believed in the visible presence of God in Indian history, particularly in "the miraculous subjugation of India by a handful of English",[133] and so they took it as their responsibility to civilize and convert the people of India to Christianity and lead them through a religious revolution similar to what the Europeans experienced at the time of the Protestant Reformation.[134] This kind of Reformation, they were convinced, could be achieved only by the introduction of Western culture. As a result, they believed, England would enjoy the benefits of commerce. The British manufacturers could not trade in India, at present, "because of the poverty of the people and unformed taste. Education and Christianity would . . . remove these obstacles."[135] Speaking in defense of the above benefits, Grant had observed,

131. See Sharp, *Selections From Education Records,* Part I, (Delhi: Published for the National Archives of India by the Manager of Publications, 1965), pp. 7-11, 19-20.
132. Muhammad Mohar Ali, *The Bengali Reaction to Christian Missionary Activities 1833-1857* (Chittagong: Mehrub Publications, 1965), p. 10.
133. Eric Stokes, *English Utilitarians and India,* pp. 30-31.
134. See Thomas Metcalf, *Aftermath of Revolt,* pp. 8-18.
135. Ibid., p. 34.

In considering the affairs of the world as under the control of the Supreme Disposer, and those distant territories . . . providentially put into our hands. . . . is it not necessary to conclude that they were given to us, not merely that *we might draw an annual profit* from them, but that we might diffuse among their inhabitants, long sunk in darkness, vice and misery, the light and benign influence of the truth, the blessings of all regulated society, the improvements and comforts of active industry? . . . In every progressive step of this work, we shall also *serve the original design with which we visited India,* that design still so important to this country - *the extension of commerce.* [Italics mine][136]

It is on this line that Grant worked for the anglicization of India. Supporting Grant, Wilberforce and the evangelicals harnessed their cause with British commercial benefits. For instance, addressing the parliament in 1813, Wilberforce said,

Let us endeavour to strike our roots into the soil by the gradual introduction of our own principles and opinions; of our laws, institutions, and manners; above all, as the source of every other improvement, of our religion, and consequently our morals. . . Are we so little aware of the vast superiority even of European laws and institutions, and far more of British institutions, over those of Asia, as not to be prepared to predict with confidence, that the Indian community which should have exchanged its dark and bloody superstitions for the genial influence of Christian light and truth, would have experienced such an increase of civil order and serenity, of social pleasures and domestic comforts, as to be desirous of preserving the blessings it should have acquired; and can we doubt that it would be bound even by the ties of gratitude to those who have been the honoured instruments of communicating them?[137]

Wilberforce continued to hold the view that humanitarian and charitable aid to Indian people would benefit Britain's commerce

---

136. Charles Grant *Observations,* p. 220.
137. Quoted in Eric Stokes, *English Utilitarians and India,* p. 35.

and evangelistic mission. He summarized his opinion when he said in 1789, "We shall soon find the rectitude of our conduct rewarded, by the benefits of a regular and growing commerce."[138]

Wilberforce's vision of commerce subserving the spread of the Good News was shared by mission societies and evangelical leaders as well in the eighteenth and nineteenth century. His argument of legitimate trade was symbolized by the Evangelical Anglicans of the Clapham Sect which advocated the founding of the Sierra Leone Company in Africa in 1790. The purpose of the formation of the Company was, Thomas Clarkson relates, "[for] the abolition of the slave trade, the civilization of Africa and the introduction of the Gospel there." Melvill Horne was sent as a chaplain to fulfill the evangelical's vision.[139] This view of colony's function to serve commerce and gospel was shared by missionaries of other denominations as well. William Carey wrote in *An Enquiry*, trade with colonies will benefit the church and the spreading of the gospel.

In spite of the enormous support received from the public and fiery debates won in the parliament, the proposed assimilation of commerce and missionary work could not take place in 1813. The evangelicals had to lobby for another twenty years and wait for the emergence of a new generation of leadership under Zachary Macaulay's son, Thomas Babington Macaulay. Commenting on the prevalent opinion of the people and politicians of this period, Eric Stokes wrote,

> Commercial and missionary opinion were agreed upon the fundamentals of the Indian problem and its solution. Together they generated the colonial policy of the nineteenth century liberalism. This was the policy of the anglicizing movement. Because of the close connexion of Grant and Teignmouth with the Company, the alliance of missionary and commercial opinion did not occur in 1813, but by the early eighteen-twenties these groups were rapidly fusing. This was part of a wider process by which Evangelical and non-Conformist opinion abandoned its toryism of the Napoleonic war era and went over to the side of reform. It can be best seen in the second

138. *Parliamentary Register*, XXVI (1789), p. 150.
139. cited in Brian Stanley, *The Bible and the Flag*, p. 70.

generation of the Clapham group. The younger Charles Grant, who in 1813 had delivered one of the finest speeches of his day in defence of the Company . . . passed over to the Whig side, and was the minister for framing the Bill which finally brought the commercial functions of the Company to an end in 1833.[140]

Grant was joined by Thomas Macaulay and together they succeeded in achieving free trade and provision for the missionaries' presence in India. Thus began the alliance of commercial endeavor and political activities of the government with the missionary enterprise of the evangelicals in England during the second quarter of the nineteenth century.

Nineteenth Century Mission and Colonial Monetrism

The history of indigo-plantation constitutes one of the dark chapters of British rule in India. George Watt in *The Commercial Products of India* wrote, "The story of the indigo industry is more interesting historically and more pathetically instructive than that of almost any other Indian agricultural or industrial substance."[141]

To a post-colonial historian the indigo industry is painfully significant for additional reasons. The history of indigo industry can be traced back not only to the violent exploitation of the colonizers but also to the missionaries' association with the indigo planters. It laid the foundation for the monetary investment of the British people in India, and for the intertwining of colonial monetrism and missionary evangelism.

The history of the indigo industry in India is a history of terror, exploitation, and fear. Testifying against the planters, E.Delatour, a liberal-minded magistrate of Faridpur, India in 1860, said before the Indigo Commission, "There is one thing more I wish to say; that considerable odium has been thrown on the missionaries for saying that 'not a chest of indigo reached England without being stained with human blood.' That expression is mine and I adapt it in the fullest and broadest

---

140. Ibid., p. 40.
141. George Watt, *The Commercial Products of India: The Dictionary of the Economic Products of India* (London: J. Murray, 1908), p. 668.

sense of its meaning."[142]

The British inherited the trade from the Portuguese and Dutch and made it a most profitable business. As early as the seventeenth century, the Company earned over 400 percent profit on its investment in indigo trade.[143] Having found indigo to be a profitable trade, the Company after 1788 gave monetary support to the European planters in North Bengal and Bihar.[144] By the end of the eighteenth century, with the help of John Shore and the monetary assistance to the planters, the indigo plantation became booming business and the Directors were able to acknowledge, "It supplies much of the consumption of Europe, and no rival to it seems to arise; it will, therefore, probably continue to be largely in demand."[145]

However, the Company sought the protection of Lord Wellesley to guard them against the potential interference of new competitors. To that effect, no one from Europe was allowed to enter into India without the permission of the Company, and thus a trade monopoly was established. This practice continued until the Charter Act of 1813, which ended the trade monopoly of the Company and legalized missionary work.

Over the course of time the planters began to acquire large portions of lands from the ryots (cultivators) and zamindars (rich landlords) on temporary and permanent lease with the enormous sum of money they had made in the trade. The lease period was anywhere from sixty to one hundred years. With their power and privilege, they drew objectionable contracts and agreements with the ryots and forced them to cultivate indigo on their fields. In 1823 Lord Amherst, the Governor General, favored the planters by granting legal power to sue the land-owners and confiscate their land if they failed to comply with the contract. Through the Regulation Act V of 1829, which helped the planters to take the

---

142. *Indigo Commission Report,* Microfilm, Reel No. 76. Also See Nil Durpan, (ed) *Sudhi Pradhan,* (Calcutta, n.d.), p. vi.

143. Shafaat Ahmad Khan, *The East India Trade in the Seventeenth Century in its Political and Economic Aspects* (London, Oxford: Oxford University Press, 1923), pp. 12, 158.

144. Holden Ferber, *John Company at Work* (Cambridge, 1951), p. 291.

145. Proceedings of the Board of Trade, 28 October 1796, Central State Archive of Calcutta, quoted in S.K. Mittal, *Peasant Uprisings and Mahatma Gandhi in North Bihar* (Meerut: Anu Prakashan, 1978), p. 8.

law into their own hands, William Bentinck granted planters the right to prosecute and imprison the ryots if they failed to follow the contract in its letter.

Through Act V, Bentinck encouraged European planters to settle in the countryside and carry on the trade. He was convinced that the European presence in the countryside would civilize the people and eventually lead them to embrace Christianity. The occasional misconduct and excess of the planters, he said, was fully outweighed by the benefits they brought to the people. This sentiment was agreed to by the parliamentary Select Committee that prepared the Charter Act of 1833. The Charter made possible the unhindered flow of European immigrants and missionaries and removed all traces of trade monopoly.[146]

The Committee also enhanced the power of the Governor General in Council and recommended that admission of Europeans into the countryside be carefully monitored. The Charter Act created a Law Commission to enquire into the courts and the operation of the laws, and appointed Thomas Macaulay as the head of the Commission and the Legal Members of the Governor General's Legislative Council. As an advocate of westernization and a believer in utilitarian philosophy, Macaulay believed that the government should administer justice to all, particularly to the *ryots*. He wrote in one of his Minutes, "That great evils exist, that great injustice is frequently committed, that many ryots have been brought – partly by the operation of the law and partly by acts committed in defiance of the law – into a state not very far removed from that of slavery, I fear, is too certain."[147]

By introducing law and legislation, Macaulay was trying to redress the agony caused by the planters. However, the indigo planters continued to enslave the *ryots*, and the cultivators were "yearning to breathe free." R.C.Majumdar, in fact, summarizes the cruelty of this dark period in *The History and Culture of the Indian People*.

---

146. Blair B. Kling, *The Blue Mutiny* (Philadelphia: University of Pennsylvania Press, 1966), p. 44.
147. C.D. Dharker, ed., *Lord Macaulay's Legislative Minutes* (London, Oxofrd: Oxford University Press, 1946), p. 272.

That the cultivation of indigo was not voluntary on the part of the *ryot;* that he was compelled to plough, sow, and weed his land, and to cut and cart the plant at times when he would prefer being engaged in other agricultural work of superior profit; that the land devoted to indigo was selected by the servants of the planters, was chosen best land very often, and was sometimes forcibly ploughed up to be resown with indigo when it was already sown with other crops; that the cultivation was thus rendered irksome and harassing to the *ryot;* that he invariably became indebted to the factory and was obliged to bequeath his debts to his descendants which almost deprived them of personal freedom; that he was oppressed by the servants of the factory, kidnapped, imprisoned and outraged; that the planters used unjustifiable means to obtain estates in *patini* from the *zamindars;* and that the system generally was vicious in theory, injurious in practice and radically unsound.[148]

It is nearly impossible for Asian historians to comprehend the irony and duplicity that have been flaunted in European political and mission history. The evangelical Christians who fought fervently against slavery in Britain faltered when analyzing the underlying usurpation of British rule in India. The evangelicals were convinced that the hand of God was at work in favor of them and that they should save souls from worshipping idols, the enemy of God.

Furthermore, the Indian religious and social system was so intriguing to the Western mind that they looked at the native population from biased position and judged them with queer and stereotypical images. Commenting on the attitudes of Carey and his colleagues, Stanley writes:

Carey and his colleagues longed and prayed for the destruction of the caste system, and its replacement by a society with no artificial barriers to stand in the way of conversion to Christ. Their initial evaluation of the Indian national character was negative: [Carey wrote] 'Avarice and servility are so joined in, I think, every individual, that cheating, juggling, and lying,

---

148. R.C. Majumdar, *British Paramountcy and India Renaissance,* p. 918.

are esteemed as no sins with them.' Like countless Western missionaries of a later generation, the BMS pioneers interpreted as innate deceitfulness the Oriental propensity to give in conversation the answer which is known to be desired, rather than that which corresponds to the objective 'facts', as a Westerner would perceive them.[149]

William Carey and Colonial Monetrism

William Carey, the first self-sponsored Baptist Missionary from England, arrived in the Hooghly in November 1793. His missionary work in India was anything but auspicious. He had to reside in India inconspicuously since he had no permit from the Company. The money and goods that he brought from England were mismanaged by Thomas, a fellow worker, leaving Carey and his family in a desperate plight. After a couple of months of living on charity, Thomas had renewed an old acquaintance with George Udny, an indigo manufacturer in North Bengal. Udny offered both Carey and Thomas jobs as managers of two of his newly established indigo factories in Malda District. Carey considered the offer a Divine Providence and moved to Madnabati in Malda district in June 1794. In spite of the loss of one of Carey's sons and the chronic sickness of his wife, Madnabati became their home for the next five and a half years.

The plantation position helped Carey establish closer touch with the workers from whom he learned the Bengali and Sanskrit languages. The ninety and more workers who were under him were so poor that they were forced to depend upon the plantation owners. This gave Carey the positional advantage to use the workers as his congregation. The European planters and administrators considered the people human material to be used for personal and collective profit; the missionaries considered the people unregenerate, uncivilized pagans who were to be converted to a particular mode of religion. There was no decisive shift in the paradigm of the primacy of European civilization and Western culture proposed by the power brokers in England and adopted by their followers in India.

Carey was contented with the work he was doing as a manager of the plantation. He was making an enormous amount of money

---

149. Brian Stanley, *The Bible and The Flag*, p. 159.

as a manager of the indigo factory. When Udny had to get rid of the factories after disastrous floods, Carey bought one of the factories and made plans to establish a community on the model of the Moravian Brethren. It was then that four families from England arrived in the Hooghly on an American ship. Since they had no permission from the Company to reside in India, they moved to Serampore, a Danish colony fifteen miles upstream from Calcutta.[150] When Carey heard about it, he sold the factory and went down to join them at Serampore. Thus began the Serampore Mission.

Carey's only motive in India was to learn the local languages and convert the Indian people. He made no effort to preach to the unconverted Europeans on the Indian soil. He was a beneficiary of the colonial structure, in spite of his initial trouble with the colonizers. The British evangelical missionaries' concern during Carey's era was to save souls from perdition. Their relationship to external forces was to them only a matter of secondary importance.

Although the natives were exploited in the indigo factories with poor salaries and long hours of work, Carey was willing to take up the job as a manager because of his desperate need and the high pay the European managers were being offered. As a European, Carey was given the job as a manager and paid "two hundred rupees per month, and commission upon all the indigo that was sold and . . . a share in the works."[151] He wrote to the society in England that he was "amply provided for" by the indigo factory and asked them to stop his allowance.[152] He believed that the job in the indigo factory was God's way of guiding him in an alien land, and he continued his work as a manager for five years.[153] Carey was convinced that the work would help him fulfil his missionary obligation as well as family commitment. His expressed wish was that "the mission may be abundantly forwarded by having a number of the natives under my immediate inspection." At the same time, his family would also be "well provided for."[154]

---

150. William Carey, *Memoir* (Boston: Gould, Kendell and Lincoln, 1836), p. 235.
151. Ibid., p. 121.
152. Ibid., p. 131.
153. Ibid., p. 135.
154. Ibid., p. 105.

In contrast, the native workers who labored under him from sun rise to sun set at the Indigo factories were paid anywhere from two and a half rupees to four rupees a month.[155] When Fountain, a missionary from England, arrived Carey wrote that a single person would need at least sixty rupees a month to have his basic needs met.[156]

Before he arrived in India, Carey was imbued with North American theology, and President Jonathan Edwards was his favored author. He wanted to exemplify the sufferings of David Brainerd in his life. Carey's humble origin, the sufferings of his childhood and adult life, brought him closer to God. However, Carey's character shows a limited perspective for a less privileged but violently colonized people, and his lack of interest to speak on behalf of the economically victimized.

At the later part of his ministry Carey did stand against the social evils of the day which were sanctioned by the Hindu religious hierarchy upon the adherents of Hindu religion, particularly, Carey did fight against Sati (widow burning) and child-sacrifice. He did encourage the British-India government to pass laws against such social practices which were imposed upon the Hindu populace as sacred religious duties. In spite of Carey's lofty social and moral ideals in delivering the innocent victims from cruel religious practices, Carey had miserably failed from raising his voice against European political and economic oppression in India. His fight against Hindu social and religious evils had evangelistic and missionizing goals. Carey's unwillingness to speak against the political and economic evils of the colonial government had missional and monetary aims. Carey failed to grasp the colonial structure under which mission was nourished. After Carey's death, a few missionaries spoke against the woeful condition in which the Indian workers were laboring in Indigo plantation and the sinister practices followed by the plantation owners in annexing the properties of the native landlords.[157] The dissenting voice came late for rescue. By then the plantation business was beginning to lose its monopoly in Europe.

---

155. Ibid., p. 124.
156. Ibid., p. 187.
157. See Geoffrey A. Oddie, *Social Protest in India: British Protestant Missionaries and Social Reform, 1850-1900,* (New Delhi: Manohar, 1979).

Furthermore, Carey's belief in Baptist doctrines apparently contradicted his deeds on Indian soil. The Baptists believed in the separation of church and state. The church, in their view, was an association of like-minded believers who ruled without any ecclesiastical or secular head. The church cannot be used as the secular arm of the state. The state has to regulate the moral affairs of the society while the church directs the spiritual aspects of the community. In areas where church and state collide, the church holds firm. In a real sense, for a Baptist missionary who believed in the separation of state and church to take up a job under the state as a professor of Indian languages and to work as a missionary, was to act contrary to his beliefs and the polity of the Baptist church.

Soon Lord Wellesly, the Governor-General from 1798 to 1805, appointed Carey as teacher of Bengali language, and in 1801 as professor of both Bengali and Sanskrit languages, in the College of Fort William at Calcutta. Carey did not hesitate to accept the assignment. He was of the opinion that the job would bring him an enormous amount of money to do missionary work.

> Until lately I was teacher of three languages in the college, on a monthly salary of five hundred rupees per month; but on the 1st of January past, I was, by the governor-general in council, appointed professor of the Sanscrit and Bengali languages, to which Mahratta is added, though not specified in the official letter, with a salary of one thousand rupees per month. *This will much help the mission.*[158] [Italics mine]

Even the Baptist Missionary Society back in England did not feel any infringement upon the polity of the Society, since Carey worked at the Fort Williams College, which trained the administrators of the colonial government and helped the missionaries further the mission by purchasing books printed at Serampore press and by providing Carey a substantial salary. This combination of power and knowledge set the missionary enterprise on a steady keel even during stormy days.

Carey was paid one thousand rupees per month by the Governor-General for teaching and training the imperial

---

158. Ibid., p. 330.

administrators in the knowledge of Indian languages. His salary was charged to the British-India government's general expenses which they collected through taxes and revenues from the people of India. In short, Carey was able to carry on the work of the Serampore Mission with the money he received from the British-India government's treasury for training the imperial rulers.[159]

In his book *Colonialism and Christian Missions*, Stephen Neill mourns that the European missionaries were poorly paid and paid far less than what their secular counterparts were making in government jobs.[160] In this context, Carey was being paid one thousand rupees per month, comparable to any other high-ranking administrative officer for his part-time job. During Carey's days, the salary of an average, full-time Indian worker was only four rupees a month. Even after almost two hundred years, the salary of an average full time presbyter in the Church of South India was not one thousand rupees. The British India government's willingness to pay Carey such a large amount of money for his part-time job, and the missionary's voluntary giving of ninety per cent of his income to the Serampore Mission, point to the subtle, yet unconscious way in which colonial monetrism was put to use in furthering colonial mission activities.

A structural missiological counterpart of Carey, Christian Schwartz, on the other hand, was able to accomplish his missionary efforts with a different approach. Almost fifty years before Carey arrived in India, Schwartz was working in South India in the court of the king of Tanjore as an administrator for which he was known as "the royal priest of Tanjore."[161] He was an able diplomat and a loyal worker for king Tulajee of Thanjavur. Like Carey, he knew Portuguese, Persian, Urdu, Marathi, English, Hindustani, Arabic, Tamil, and several other European languages. He established several churches along the southeast coast of India with his own funds. He even served as a go-between, when Haider Ali allied himself with the French and meditated war against the British. Schwartz was a trusted friend of all people.

---

159. See R.C. Majumdar, *British Parmountcy and Indian Renaissance*, pp. 356-401.
160. Stephen Neill, *Colonialism and Christian Missions* (London: McGraw Hill Book Company, 1966), p. 38.
161. Stephen Neill, *A History of Christianity in India 1707-1848* (Cambridge: Cambridge University Press, 1985), p. 49.

Even at the height of the Carnatic war, Haider Ali asked for Schwartz to represent the hostile British government by saying, "Let them send me the Christian; he will not deceive me."[162]

On his death bed, King Tulajee asked Schwartz to take his adopted son Saroboji and raise him. When Saroboji himself succeeded the throne, he wrote a memorable letter to the East India Company about Schwartz' death, "Oh, Gentlemen, that you were but able to send missionaries who should resemble the departed Schwartz!"[163] The king inscribed his gratitude on the tomb in Tanjore, "My father, my friend, the protector and guardian." A church in Tanjore, South India still bears the love of Saroboji that has been carved permanently on a granite with poetic skill. "May. . . my father, be worthy of thee, Wisheth and prayeth Saroboji."[164]

It was this kind of missionary work that has always been admired and appreciated by the people in India. The Serampore Mission was carried out with colonial monetrism and with the help of the colonial government. The Western mission scholars' reference to one of their former missionaries as "the father of modern missions" needs to be redefined.

The mission literature written by Western scholars is replete with such undue canonization. My argument is that mission literature is multiphonal and contains ruptures and discontinuities, as Foucault's theory points out, and hence the text has to be reevaluated in the light of post-independence India's political, social, and historical consciousness. In short, the texts need to be decolonized.

After 1813, the missionaries were not only given free access to territories under British rule, but also were sometimes actively encouraged to expand their operations in certain directions. In 1813 the Resident of the Molucca Islands suggested to Lord Moira[165] that the people in those islands would enjoy "the benefits of true religion" if the Serampore Mission could establish an extension school in the area. Moira supported the idea and promised to

---

162. Cyril B. Firth, *An Introduction to Indian Church History* (Madras: The Christian Literature Soceity, 1961), p. 137.
163. Arthur Mayhew, *Christianity and the Government of India*, p. 31.
164. Ibid.
165. Later he was known as Lord Hastings the Governor General of India.

extend every assistance to the Mission if it would choose to go.[166]
Lord Moira also visited the Serampore Mission headquarters
and the printing plant in 1815, and placed orders for an enormous
number of copies of Sanskrit and other literatures printed at the
Serampore press.[167] When William Ward addressed the Wesleyan
Missionary Society in London in 1821, he summarized the trio's
relationship with the colonial government: "The Government of
India acts, as far as is prudent, entirely with us; and in a variety
of ways, they are assisting us, and assisting us in the most powerful
manner."[168]

166. Ernest Alexander Payne, *South-East from Serampore* (London: The Carey
Press, 1945), p. 16.
167. Sophia, the Marchioness of Bute (ed.,), *The Private Journal of the Marquess of Hastings*, 2nd ed. (London: Saunders and Otley, 1858) pp. ii, 94.
168. Quoted in *The Missionary Register*, May 1821, p. 179.

CHAPTER V

English Education and Colonial Missiography

Two major factors that exerted a decisive influence upon missionary work in India during the second quarter of the nineteenth century were approval of the permanent presence of missionaries in India through the Charter Act of 1833, and the legalization of English education in 1835. Evangelicals in England and missionaries in India were the prime movers behind these changes. With their ceaseless propaganda, the evangelicals brought about a change in the political climate in England, and missionaries effected a similar transformation in the administrative structure in India.

Missionaries and mission societies were convinced that Western education would bring religious transformation and cultural revolution in Indian society and thus prepare the way for evangelization of India. The general tone of this missionary era was to strive for a rudimentary change in non-Christian communities. Stanley summarizes the mood of the missionaries:

> The content of their [missionaries] hope was not merely a conglomerate of individual conversions but a comprehensive revolution in 'heathen' society in which every aspect of that society would be praised from the grip of satanic dominion and submitted to the liberating lordship of Christ.[169]

Trusting in the transcendent power of Western education and the universality of English literature, missionaries often ignored some of the burning issues of the day and were concerned only about civilizing and christianizing people in India. For instance, Duff and his colleagues had the dream of destroying the religious system of the nation and introducing Western education to promote a Copernican revolution in religious and cultural life of the people of India. Duff's underlying assumption was that nineteenth century Britain was a paradigm of Christian culture and society. His

---

169. Brian Stanley, *The Bible and the Flag,* p. 75.

strong presumption was that Christianity, as revealed in the Bible and firmly established by the Protestant Reformation, had made Britain unparalleled in history. The existing colonial structure served as an acolyte to light the dreams of missionaries on Indian soil.

Before I discuss in detail the work of the missionary educators and their societies, let me briefly summarize the prevalent mood and distinguishing traits of nineteenth-century missionary societies in India. The desire for the conversion of Indian people to Christian faith was absolutized to such an extent that its limitation by the rights of the people and the needs of the Indian community was not kept in mind.

The customs, the traditions, and the religious beliefs of the people were considered the very signs of the depravity and futility of the people. For instance, speaking to the Parliament, William Wilberforce argued that the introduction of European enlightenment would prepare the people for conversion to Christianity.

When truth and reason so long excluded from that benighted land shall once more obtain an access to it . . . the understanding of the natives will begin to exert their powers; and their minds once more enlightened, will instinctively reject the profane absurdities of their theological and the depraving vices of their moral system. Thus they will be prepared for the reception of Christianity.[170]

Wilberforce's sentiment was shared by other missionaries as well. A missionary educator in South India said that European education would plant the seeds for the conversion and civilizing of the natives. He reasoned, "When these children are early instructed in the principles of religion, I hope they will make a due application of them when they come to manhood, and their national ignorance and superstition will then cease and the success of our present exertions for civilizing and evangelizing them will be apparent."[171]

Civilizing and Christianizing the colonized went together and formed the highest of missionary goals. Evangelizing and educating

---

170. *Parliamentary Debates*, vol. 26 (1813), p. 1076.
171. *Missionary Register* for 1819, p. 104.

the people formed part of the same balance-sheet.[172] Having thus made mission activity into an "Ersatz" religion, missionaries were intent on promoting the political and administrative advantages of their presence. Instead of relying on the absolute, transforming power of the Gospel alone, missionaries strove to ensure success through colonial means and methods. Both the colonizers and the mission societies felt the need for the permanent presence of the Empire. Being a missionary in India became an acceptable norm of the colonial structure and an accessible means to gain some converts to the crown. In this way Christian missionary work was rendered useful and existential.

The Gospel had not exerted its holistic influence on the Indian populace. In its place, Western science and education, and benefits of higher culture, were thrust upon India. Mission's role was shrunk to mere destruction of pagan religion and establishment of a civilized community in the Western order.

In a similar way, British administrators had to depend upon missionaries for their expertise in understanding local language, culture, and customs of the people. Since British government's survival in India rested mainly on the ability to secure information about the people whom the government was managing, their power, knowledge, and politics required constant interaction with the people and mission societies.

Missionaries were able to aid the government by providing useful advice and information which not only became informative but also operative. The Mutiny of 1857 forced the colonials to realize that force alone would not serve the purpose. In its place they resorted to coercion and conciliation. This interdependence was aptly described by Frantz Fannon in *The Wretched of the Earth*. He says, "The triumphant *communiques* from the missions are in fact a source of information concerning the implantation of foreign influences in the core of the colonized people. The church in the colonies is the white people's church, the foreign church. She does not call natives to God's ways but to the ways of the white man, of the master, of the oppressor."[173]

The formal and informal networks which had been established

---

172. See Bruce McCully, *English Education*, pp. 12-18, 41ff.
173. Frantz Fannon, *The Wretched of the Earth*, trans. Constance Farrington, (New York: Grove Press, 1963), p. 34.

in the bureaucracy facilitated flow of information. Different modes of communication networks which the British used brought in the "native opinion" of the British presence. The administration's alliance with the linguists, philologists, orientalists, and missionaries played a vital role in governmental decision-making. Since the colonizers wanted to rule the country peacefully, implementation of political and administrative decisions had to be carefully weighed in a delicate balance of the nationals' acceptance or rejection. Regional mutiny, rebellion, and hostility made the administration vulnerable. The government relied on information from missionaries and all conceivable sources for the survival of the empire. Since missionaries knew the local languages, culture, and "character" of the people, missionaries had the advantage of being source persons for the British Raj.

The evangelical sympathies, fed by the Clapham Sect, Wilberforce, Grant, Udny, Thornton, Zachary Macaulay, and others, began to make people in England realize that they had a moral obligation to the social, intellectual and ethical development of the people of India. For instance, Charles Grant wrote in *Observations,*

> The true cure of darkness is, the introduction of light. The Hindoos err, because they are ignorant and their errors have never fairly been laid before them. The communication of our light and knowledge to them, would prove the best remedy for their disorders; and this remedy is proposed from a full conviction that if judiciously and patiently applied it would have great and happy effects upon them, effects honourable and advantageous for us.[174]

This and similar kinds of arguments by other evangelicals resulted in the introduction of the pious clause in the Charter of 1813, and the approval of the permanent presence of the missionaries in the Charter of 1833. The common denominator between missionaries and the colonials after 1833 became the introduction of learning, the primary agent of civilization.[175] The government hoped that education would civilize the natives so as

---

174. Charles Grant, *Observations,* p. 734.
175. Bruce McCully, *English Education,* p. 160.

to facilitate better business transactions; missionaries envisioned that it would reduce the pagan religions to nothing and pave the way for the dissemination of Christian faith. Thus began another round of collaboration between mission and colonialism.[176]

English Education and Longevity of the Empire: Two Contextual Developments

After the Charter of 1833 was renewed, missionaries were allowed freely to be present, and free trade was established. Missionary force became powerful and took a different turn. Unlike Carey, a new breed of missionaries began to arrive. Those missionaries were supported by churches and individuals in England which were influential in character.[177] Soon, through letters, reports, and stories, missionaries created an image in England about the people and culture of India. The doctrine that was sold by them was that civilizing and Christianizing should go together; it is the moral responsibility of the government to support all Christian values and the government should not encourage the traditional religious practices. Thomas R. Metcalf summarized the demands of missionaries when he wrote, "The missionaries asserted that since God had laid upon Britain the solemn duty of evangelizing India, the Government should not hesitate to throw its weight into the struggle. They demanded above all open Government patronage of Christian education and vigorous warfare upon the abuses associated with the Hindu religion."[178] Moreover, when English education was introduced in India, Alexander Duff reasoned that mere introduction of Western science into academia was value-neutral, or amoral; it should include moral and ethical teachings, by which he meant Christian instructions.

If the government had to make a choice between Hindu/ Muslim religions and Christianity, missionaries argued, the government should choose the latter. This proposed open alliance

---

176. See Thomas Metcalf, *Aftermath of Revolt*, pp. 12ff.
177. E. J. Rapson, "Charles Grant," *Dictionary of National Biography*, ed., Leslie Stephen & Sidney Lee, vol. 22 (New York: 1890), pp. 378-380. Also, Syed Mahmood, *A History of English Education in India, 1789-1893*, (India: Aligarh, 1895), p. 3.
178. Thomas Metcalf, *Aftermath of Revolt*, p. 25.

was practiced by Lord Wellesly and Lord Bentinck.[179] When Lord Auckland tried to adopt the policy of neutrality, he was violently opposed.

For instance, when Lord Auckland supported the Hindu Jaggernauth temple and Muslim mosques with a pilgrim tax, Duff wrote a lengthy letter saying that Lord Auckland's face would be rubbed in England's public mud unless he stopped supporting the Indian idolatrous and religious practices. Duff shared the prevalent sentiment of his time: Idolatry is the worst sin of Heathenism. In 1858 the *Wesleyan Methodist Magazine* gave a reason for missionary enterprise and a reason to put an end to idolatry.

> The most serious controversy that ever rose between God and man is represented in the system of idolatry. In every idol we see God's rival. In every idolater we see a man who takes against God, and supports a system which involves the rankest injustice toward God.[180]

In his enthusiasm Duff started a crusade against idolatry, and reduced all religions except Christianity to idolatry. In what proved to be a memorable letter, Duff derided Lord Auckland, the top British administrator in India, and made his reputation boom and crash in the imaginary ecclesiastical and political stock exchange for his support of the Hindu temple. He observed in early 1841 in his letter to Lord Auckland:

> British public, and above all, religious public in Great Britain, which heretofore hath been moved, and may readily be moved again, by the addresses and expostulations of a Christian missionary. It was the righteous agitation of this public which wrenched asunder the bars of the prohibition to the ingress of Bibles and heralds of salvation into India. It was the righteous agitation of this public which accelerated and insured the abolition of the murderous rite of suttee. It was the righteous agitation of this public which foredoomed the ultimate severance of official British connection with the mosques and temples

---

179. Bruce McCully, *English Education*, pp. 17ff.
180. *Wesleyan Methodist Magazine*, II (1856), p. 894.

and idolatrous observances of this benighted people. And rest
assured, my lord, . . . as a blot and disgrace, . . . your lordship
has restored the government patronage and support to the
shrines and sanctuaries of Hindoo and Muhammodan learning
with all their idolatrous, pantheistic errors! A surer prospect
of earning the garland of victory no Christian missionary could
possibly desire, than the opportunity of boldly confronting,
on a theme like this, the mightiest of our state functionaries,
in the presence of a promiscuous audience of British-born
free-man, in any city or district, from Cornwall to Shetland.[181]

What we observe here is the missionary's unfamiliarity with
Muslim religion. Duff considers Islam an "idolatrous, pantheistic"
religion, which it is not. He offers to the readers "a passage to
India" that is pure *tableau vivanti* in the manner of the orientalists.
We do not see any deeper entrance beyond the series of queer
images he borrowed from the colonizers. The "benighted people"
are the cultural and religious opposite of European rationality,
Western possibility, and Evangelical spirituality. And so, Duff
argues that the primitive Indian culture should be exorcised,
religious ignorance cast out, and people "ṣanctified" from their
evil religions by imposing English education upon them. Like
early missionaries, philologists, and orientalists, Duff also sees
the abnormalities of India, in contrast to Europe and its rationality,
and suggests that the introduction of Western science and
Christianity alone would redeem the people from their cultural
pathos.

Duff's strong belief in European superiority and political
ideology characterizes what David Lochhead calls the theology of
nineteenth-century colonial missionaries, the "theology of
isolation."[182] Duff was not alone in isolating the people of non-
Western societies and positioning them at the lowest rung of
civilization. His predecessor, Carey, wrote in *An Enquiry* that all
non-Western societies are culturally inferior. The antidote to
religious ignorance and cultural lowliness is preaching of the
Gospel and introduction of superior Western culture. While

181. George Smith, *The Life of Alexander Duff,* (New York: American Tract
Society, n. d.), p. 435.
182. David Lochhead, *The Dialogical Imperative,* (New York: Orbis Books,
1988), pp. 8-14.

defending the necessity of foreign mission, Carey expressed his feelings about the superiority of European culture.

It has been objected that there are multitudes in our nation, and within our immediate spheres of action who are as ignorant as the South sea savages, and that therefore we have work enough at home, without going into other countries. That there are thousands in our land as far from God as possible, I readily grant, and that this ought to excite us to ten-fold diligence in our work, and in attempts to spread divine knowledge amongst them is a certain fact; but that it ought to supersede all attempts to spread the gospel in foreign parts seems to want proof. Our own country men have the means of grace, and may attend on the word preached if they choose it. They have the means of knowing the truth, and faithful ministers are placed in almost every part of the land, whose spheres of action might be much extended if their congregations were but more . . . active in the cause: but with them the case is different, who have no Bible, no written language, . . . no ministers no good civil government, nor any of those advantages, which we have. Pity therefore, humanity, and much more Christianity, call loudly for every possible exertion to introduce the gospel amongst them.[183]

While he followed the policies of his predecessors, Duff, unlike Carey and others, was able to appeal to a wider public with his letters, lectures and political connections. In his enthusiasm to missionize the people, unfortunately, the missionary speaks the pure language of the colonizers. He does not lighten the already existing oppression; nor does he seek to hide the domination. With clear conscience, he reveals them. As an upholder of European superiority, he encourages the government to practice a national program of intellectual and spiritual colonization.

What is evident is a Western missionary who failed to see beyond his European experience but had the epistemological privilege of evaluating the materiality of a subcontinent. The positional superiority he was endowed with as a European helped

---

183. William Carey, *An Enquiry into the Obligations of Christians to Use Means for the Conversion of the Heathen* (Leicester, 1792), 13.

him summon the colonial power to aid his missionary endeavor, and to make decisions on behalf of what appeared to him a weaker and less developed non-European society.

The missionary's sense of religious and cultural superiority was, in fact, typical of his period. After 1800 industrialized Britain was considered culturally and civilizationally an advanced nation. India was consigned to the lowest rung of the ladder of civilization because of its "barbarous and superstitious" religious practices. Missionaries and the colonists argued that the country could be saved only through a "complete reformation."[184] In his influential books *Representative Government* and *Dissertations and Discussions*, John Stuart Mill commented that the barbaric, sub-human beings in India can be brought to the level of human-beings only through "parental despotism" and training in Western knowledge. Once a person is introduced to European knowledge, he will become a "reflecting, an observing, and therefore naturally a self-governing, a moral, and a successful human being."[185]

A post-colonial critique of the Euro-centric approach is seen in Rana Kabbani's *Europe's Myths of Orient*. In this book she argues that nineteenth-century Europeans believed that Western religion and culture had all the ingredients to uplift any lowly, primitive culture. His immense belief in the "transcendent" European civilization made Duff carry out what in Napoleon's "laicized version" is called the *mission civilisatrice*."[186]

This kind of belief in European religious superiority is discussed at length in Norman Daniel's *Islam, Europe and Empire*.

The new conviction of superiority arose from technologies and techniques of government, but it took the form of a belief in Christian superiority . . . Superiority was explained as the result, not of new techniques, but of old morality: often, as though the Christian morality had been necessary to achieve the techniques. There was revived in the Victorian Age the

---

184. Metcalf, *The Aftermath of Revolt*, pp. 7-8. Also see, James Mill, *The History of British India*, vol. 2, pp. 106-167.
185. John Stuart Mill, *Representative Government*, p. 199; *Dissertations and Discussions*, vol.2, p. 282.
186. See Rana Kabbani, *Europe's Myths of Orient* (Bloomington: Indiana University Press, 1986), p. 105.

religious and moral fervour of the Middle Ages, speaking with the modern accent of material progress.[187]

Evangelical spirituality and cultural superiority were inculcated by religious authority figures. For instance, Duff's mentor, Dr.John Inglis, was the minister of old Grey Friars at Edinburgh, whose church Duff attended as he was a young man. Dr. Inglis was greatly responsible for Duff's growth in Christian character and commitment to mission. Dr. Inglis encouraged Duff to educate, to civilize, and to use commercial connection for the conversion of people in India.[188]

Duff was very meticulous in following the teachings of his spiritual guide and combined English education with economic factors. Commenting on this bread-and-butter combination, McCully summarizes the unique role Duff played.

> Blessed with a keener vision than most of his missionary compatriots, Duff fastened his gaze upon the evolving economic life that swirled through . . . (Calcutta) and saw that the struggle for employment must inevitably force native job-hunters to seek a higher type of training than elementary institutions could provide. In designing his institutions he trimmed his sails to fit that demand.[189]

This kind of missionary enterprise already involved the Church Missionary Society, the London Missionary Society, the Baptist Missionary Society, and the General Assembly of the Church of Scotland. Later, the American Board of Missions also joined.[190] Interestingly, all the English schools in India, except Banares, in India were established within 300 miles of Calcutta, the colonial powerhouse in India. The province of Bengal was the area most affected economically because of the destruction of cotton industries by the import of manufactured goods from England and the policy of free trade. To a certain extent, English education helped the native, urban elites, but a vast majority of the underprivileged

---

187. Norman Daniel, *Islam, Europe and Empire*, 246. Quoted by Rana Kabbani in *Europe's Myths of Orient*, p. 105.
188. George Smith, *Alexander Duff*, p. 37.
189. Bruce McCully, *English Education*, p. 44.
190. Ibid., pp. 46, 50.

and rural masses were left out in the shuffle.

Like their predecessors, Duff and his colleagues neither questioned nor ringingly affirmed, asserted or justified the colonizers' presence; it was simply assumed. Thus missionaries could speak almost in one breath of both the need to carry out the moral mission and the introduction of English literature which formed the materials of the Christian religion. The identity of the masterpieces of British literature was taken for granted alongside the Biblical canon and considered more appropriate for the conversion of the people.

In doing so Alexander Duff exhibits a severely limited conception of the domain of Christian Mission and the evangelistic method and its phenomena. Further, in his conceptual and methodological confinement Duff was joined by Charles Trevelyan and his brother-in-law Thomas Macaulay, and thus formed the triumvirs of English education in India.[191] Those "big three" represented India and spoke on its behalf through the voice they adopted, the structure they built, the moral ideas they projected, and the political ideas they sold.

To these triumvirs, civilizing and Christianizing were synonyms: civilizing Indian people would facilitate easy commercial intercourse; Christianizing would make them loyal to the British crown.[192] The end result could be achieved only through the introduction of Western education. The process of civilization was taken as seriously by the colonials as by missionaries. For example, casting aside the orientalists' suggestion of teaching science and humanities in both English and the vernacular in schools, Macaulay expressed his contempt and ignorance for traditional education in India. He emphasized that the introduction of Western civilization through English education would enhance trade with India. According to him, "to trade with civilized men is infinitely more profitable than to govern savages."[193]

Both Macaulay and Trevelyan believed that English education would destroy native religions and facilitate the process of prosyletization. With that confidence, Macaulay wrote to his father in 1830 that in thirty years "there would not be a single idolater"

---

191. See Thomas Metcalf, *Aftermath of Revolt,* pp. 11ff.
192. George Smith, *Alexander Duff,* p. 295.
193. Speech of Lord Babington Macaulay, *Hansard,* p. 10.

in Bengal. However, Trevelyan looked beyond Macaulay and described the economic and political benefits England would enjoy as a result of English education. He wrote that English education would promote a cultural revolution and a forward movement for the betterment of the natives and make them loyal to the Crown. Once that revolution is achieved, he wrote,

(The Indian people) will cease to desire and aim at independence on the old Indian footing. The political education of a nation must be a work time; and while it is in progress, we shall be as safe as it is possible for us to be. The natives shall not rise against us, because we shall stoop to raise them; there will be no reaction, because there will be no pressure; the energy will be fully and harmlessly employed in acquiring and diffusing European knowledge, and in naturalising European institutions.[194]

Intellectual colonization was a new phenomenon introduced to the colonized world in the second quarter of the nineteenth century. The colonizers were able to sell their ideas successfully to missionaries also. To all of them, it was the exteriority that mattered most. From exterior to interior, from trade to religion was their agenda. If the evangelistic goal was to be reached, missionaries argued, a European model of reformation should be created and introduced in India. Again, not spontaneous efforts, but mobilization of forces for the movement toward reformation was what they proposed. For instance, Duff reasoned, "What the Christian Reformation did for Europe through the Greek tongue, the Roman law and the Bible in the vernaculars, it will similarly do for India and further Asia through the English language and the British Administration."[195]

What we see here is a reversal of biblical and missiological order: not from inside to outside, but from outside to inside through an artificially created movement. This is contrary to what the evangelicals preached. They believed that only inner renewal and inner transformation, which they called being-born-again, would change a person and reform a society. The

---

194. Ibid., p. 195.
195. George Smith, *Alexander Duff*, p. 205.

missionaries were taught that the preaching of the cross, in the manner of St. Paul, was what the "pagans" needed to hear. Only the message of the cross would effect reform and regeneration in individuals and society.

Contrary to the prevalent evangelical belief and teachings, Duff argues that British government was a powerful force, sent by God to Christianize India and the government should do all in its power "for the conversion of a hundred and thirty millions of idolaters."[196] In a passionate way Duff presented his case again, when he wrote,

> As soon as some of these become converts to Christianity, through the agency already described, how totally different their tone of feeling towards existing Government? Their bowels yearned over the miseries of their countrymen. They now knew the only effectual cure. And their spontaneous feeling was, "Ah! woe be unto us, if the British Government were destroyed and the Hindoo dynasties restored! The first they would be to cut us off, and what would then become to our poor degraded country? *We pray for the permanence of the British Government, that, under the shadow of its protection, we may disseminate the healing knowledge of Christianity* among our brethren,—that knowledge which alone can secure their present welfare and immortal happiness. In like manner, and for the same reason, there are not more loyal or patriotic subjects of the British crown than the young men that compose the more advanced classes in our Institution. So clearly and strongly did this appear to many members of the present Government in India, that instead of regarding us with jealousy and suspicion as enemies, *they looked upon us as the truest friends of the British Government, the staunchest supporters of the British power.*[197] [emphasis mine]

Thus we note that the existential elements which comprised the colonial structure were being preserved intact by missionaries. By attempting to introduce English education on a national level, Duff was making history; his life was an epoch; his was the

---

196. Ibid., p. 291.
197. Ibid., pp. 294, 295.

unceasing cause: "Woe unto us if the British government were destroyed and the Hindu dynasties restored!"

Juxtaposed with Duff, torpid creatures who were wasted by superstition and laziness and obsessed by idolatrous religious beliefs form an almost inorganic background for the innovating dynamism of English education. By constantly referring to the "permanence of the British government" in India, Duff clearly indicates that he himself is an extension of the colonizing country.

Duff has separated English education as a discrete political administrative field, not only in the mechanical terms of establishing permanent trade and the administrative relationship with the people, but also in the constructive terms of civilizing natives away from their backwardness and superstition-ridden culture. The new system of education thus introduced to the people, he argued, should also incorporate moral teaching by which he meant Christian instruction. This incorporation of Christian religious instruction would evoke love and respect for the British Crown among the converts and ensure the permanence of the government.

Explaining to the colonials the advantages of English education and proposing the benefits of making converts for the longevity of the empire have been two contextual developments which have characterized the second quarter of the nineteenth century. This carried the colonial missionary enterprise a step further. In addition, by joining the colonials Duff does not hesitate to hide his conviction that his primary unit of missiological concern was not only Christianizing the natives but also maintaining the external relations with the larger life of the colonials. In this way Duff's missiology tended to go beyond the formal contours of the early principles of mission and got deeply entrenched in political soil, thus perpetuating a nineteenth-century version of missionary work with an added dimension.

Realizing the importance of the presence of colonial power to accomplish his missionary goal, Duff said that Calcutta and Bengal, the administrative headquarters of the colonial government, were like Jerusalem and Syria. The human instrument God has chosen to evangelize India and southern Asia must do its part—do it urgently and most effectively. Introduction of English education and European culture is the answer to the problems of Indian society. Speaking of this period and the urgency of the need, Smith, the biographer of Duff, summarizes:

> It was the Greek tongue and the Roman order . . . to all the race the fullness of the ages. In India the set time came with the English language, with the legislation and administration, the commerce and the civilization of the British people. The Missionary had, thus far, done his work. The Governor-General in Council must do his.[198]

Thus Duff formulated a missiology which was oriented to an historical and existential dimension in a colonized setting. As I argued earlier, the under-evaluation of Indian culture was a phenomenon of nineteenth-century Europe. Duff failed to consider Eastern culture in the broader perspective of a theology of creation and employed a methodology which allowed European cultural and political values to precede biblical and missiological principles. After all, the missionary and the colonials viewed Indian culture as variable and relative, while the essence of mission and European civilization was immutable and permanently valid.

It never occurred to Duff and his colleagues that culture is not simply a question of manners, traditions, and the external manifestation of religious practices. Culture is a question of the identity of the people; the affirmation of their legitimate selfhood deserving attention and respect. Above all, culture means power, the life-blood of a community. To negate culture is to deny power and a legitimate identity to people. By destroying culture, one destroys a nation, its people and their memorable past.

Hence, Duff's missiology became a cultural missiology rooted in power and knowledge. It has incorporated a relativised biblical theory and variable evangelical theology. By accepting the treacheries of colonization which drove people into the immortal state of otherness, Duff joined the colonizers in deciding the salvific future of the people of India and the security of the empire. As a result, Duff became the most outstanding of all missionaries to focus politico-administrative structures as the model for missiological work. He formulated a missiology of epistemological relativism which was to become the matrix of the policy of nineteenth-century missionary societies.

---

198. Ibid., pp. 176-177.

CHAPTER VI

English Education: A Hegemonic Imposition

The various forms of interdependence between mission and colonialism that I have brought out so far have considerable bearing on nineteenth-century missionary work. The traditional tendency to isolate or protect nineteenth-century missions from consideration in colonial economic terms has had the effect of mystifying the dynamics of missionary work. Mission societies have been portrayed as pure, non-utilitarian, interest-free, and, in effect, value-free agents of colonial structure. A strict accounting of any of their seemingly gratuitous activities, however, would bring us to consider their missiological utility and/or their survival value.

Since missionaries, in order to carry out their missionary goals, took into account the pre-existing essentials of the colonized society in the making, their theology should be assigned a "relational place in a dialogical system;"[199] and, since the christianizing process in India accompanied the civilizing and colonizing process with the aim of converting "the barbaric, superstitious natives who lived in darkness," I contend that mission work should be demystified of this "fetishization of native savagery an evil."[200] Since, mission texts have a function of colonization and justification, they are limited and incomplete.

Orientalists, Colonizers, and Missionaries

In the Introduction to *On the Other: Dialogue and/or Dialectics*, Robert P. Scharlemann begins with a legend, and deals with the question of dealing with the other in speech, conversation, dialogue, and so on. I believe the fable he narrates is a fitting introduction to this chapter:

---

199. Frederic Jameson, *The Political Unconscious: Narrative as a Socially Symbolic Act*, (Ithaca, New York: Cornell University Press, 1981), p. 85.
200. Abdul R. JanMohamed, "The Economy of Manichean Allegory: The Function of Racial Difference in Colonialist Literature," *Critical Inquiry*, 12, (Autumn 1985), pp. 59-87.

A legend is told of two medieval monks who had agreed that the one of them who died first would send a message from the beyond. When, in the course of time, one of the monks died, the other monk directed a message to the deceased, asking whether the beyond was like the here. To his question came the reply, *Nec taliter, nec aliter, sed totaliter aliter* (neither the same, nor different, but totally different).[201]

The major problem which the commercial traders (who later became the colonizers) as well as the missionaries had to face in India was how to comprehend the complex, opulent, and ancient religious culture in India. The multicultural, multilinguistic, and multiracial Indian society was so perplexing that the Western mind tried to analyze, codify, and reduce it to simple narratological structure. During the process, the whole question of attitude toward the other became so overwhelming that the speaking self, the subject, committed itself to transforming the other without entering into a relationship. The speaking subject represented the other, negated the difference, and sublated the otherness. The speaking subject spoke for the other and created a neat-and-tidy discourse of its own. That became the historical document: the written, articulated, and factual record.

The agents of this discourse since the Protestant Reformation have been mostly traders, missionaries, and warriors. In all Western narratives about the missionized East, a basic paradigm recurred: the civilized Christian West and the backward pagan East. The East was considered "they," not "us"; it was different, not normal. The East should be conquered, civilized and converted.

This division of Europe and India, documented both by travellers and colonizers, was inherited and enhanced by missionaries. It was later incorporated into missionary literature also.[202] The description of India in mission literature unduly stressed certain qualities and characteristics that made India different from Europe, that depicted India in a non-salvific state of otherness. Two of

---

201. Robert P. Scharlemann, *On the Other: Dialogue and/or Dialectics* (Lanham, Maryland: University Press of America, Inc, 1991), p. 1.
202. See M.C. Seymour, ed., *The Travels of Sir John Mandeville* (London: Oxford University Press, 1968); Henri Cordier, *The Book of Ser Marco Polo, the Venetian, Concerning the Kingdoms and Marvels of the East,* trans. and ed. Sir Henry Yule, (London: J. Murray, 1920).

the most strikingly dominant themes were ignorant, religious superstition and barbaric cultural backwardness.

Further, certain stereotypical characteristics were attributed to the people because of the missionaries' superficial understanding of Indian races and analysis of Indian culture. Those stereotypical traits and binary oppositions were not only textualized, but also perpetuated by the missionaries' ideological impulses. Those impulses could be noticed in the exercise of cultural hegemony.

The traditional definition of "hegemony" is domination of one state over the other. For instance, in Raymond Williams' definition of hegemony, when, in a society, the dominant classes' ideology—its world-view, class outlook, and its "lived system of meanings and values"—are imposed on subordinate classes, the former is said to exercise its hegemonic rule over the latter. This hegemonic process is further defined as the "lived domination and subordination of particular" classes.[203] This cultural process may go on within a society, or a particular society may impose this on another culture.

In the Indo-European relationship the West exercised its hegemony because of the positional superiority it had enjoyed over India. Britain and France dominated the whole of the East because they were the two great powers in the eighteenth and nineteenth centuries. Military conquests and scholarly pursuits were closely related in the act of colonization. For instance, William Jones, a servant of the East India Company, is known for his significant linguistic contribution to the study of the Indo-European language group (a family of languages comprised of Germanic languages on the Western end and Sanskrit on the Eastern side). Commenting on the works of the orientalists, Christopher Dawson says in *Christianity in East and West,*

> Towards the end of the eighteenth century, Western science took up the work of the Jesuit missionaries and began to reveal an unknown world of oriental religion and philosophy. The discovery of Sanskrit literature (by Anquetil-Duperron, Sir William Jones, Sir Charles Wilkins, and Henry Colebrooke) was one of the most epoch-making events of modern times.

---

203. Raymond Williams, *Marxism and Literature* (Oxford: Oxford University Press, 1977), p. 110.

In the West, it prepared the way for an oriental renaissance which had a profound effect on European thought, especially in Germany and France, in the first decades of the nineteenth century.[204]

However, the study of the language was not interest-free. William Jones was a judge in Calcutta (1783); his knowledge of Eastern languages was used to interpret the native laws. Philology was useful in subordinating the subject race.[205] As early as 1805, before Oxford founded its academic chair for Sanskrit in 1833, the East India Company, the administrative agency of British colonialism in India until 1857, introduced Sanskrit into the curriculum of Haileybury College "for the purpose of training civil servants." [206]

Jones reflects the use of linguistic studies, "In order to deepen Europe's acquaintance with the peoples over whom it would ultimately come to have control. Europe could now afford to study the East calmly and carefully, and as England was the chief world power, it took the lead in this."[207]

While linguistic knowledge about India was useful for British administrative presence in India, the presence of the colonizers was justified by orientalists, chaplains, missionaries, and politicians. The presence of interested missionaries, traders, and philologists helped construct an India adaptable as a tool in the hands of the colonizers. For instance, commenting on the introduction of English education in India by Macaulay's Minute of 1835, Edward Said says, "[Macaulay's] decision to impose the medium of English on the subcontinent of India was based on the critical evaluation of the Orientalists."[208]

---

204. Christopher Dawson, *Christianity in East and West,* ed. John J. Mulloy (Lassalle, Illinois: Sherwood Sugden & Co., 1981), p. 37.
205. Along with these Orientalists, we can also add the nineteenth-century Orientalists such as Burnoff, Lassen, Prinsep, John Wilson, H.H. Wilson, Weber, Max Muller and the Muir brothers; and philologists like Frank Popp and, Jacob Grimm whose researches and publications aided both mission and colonization. Also see, George Smith, *Alexander Duff,* pp. 200, 375.
206. Raymond Schawb, *The Oriental Renaissance,* p. 74. This was what I argued in the last chapter, explaining how William Carey profited from his knowledge of Indian languages, particularly Sanskrit and Marathi, was cashed in by training the colonial administrators at Fort William College at Calcutta.
207. Rana Kabbani, *Europe's Myths of Orient,* p. 138.
208. Edward Said, *Orientalism,* p. 12.

What is more significant here is the seemingly disinterested attitude of Macaulay. It seems as though the issue at hand deals with the relative merit of textbooks for the cultures concerned. In his statement power is made invisible. Power seeks invisibility. In his representation of the facts of India and its less meritorious texts, and of the West and its superior quality of texts, the power of Macaulay as a political agent of imperialism is made available. While the introduction of English education appears to be benign and congenial, concerned only with for the betterment of the colonized, English is made an administrative tool to "create a class of half-breeds" who, as Macaulay himself confessed, would serve as "interpreters between us and the millions we govern; a class of persons Indian in blood and colour, but English in taste, in opinions, in morals, and in intellect."[209]

Further, with characteristic honesty Macaulay did not hesitate to betray his contempt for Indian culture and traditional learning. On his voyage from England to Calcutta he engrossed himself in Greek and Roman classics, but would not lay his hand upon a single Oriental work.[210] His contempt for Eastern literature crystallized when he uttered, "I am quite ready to take the Oriental learning at the valuation of the Orientalists themselves. I have never found one among them who could deny that a single shelf of good European library was worth the whole native literature of India and Arabia."[211]

Thus, after deriding Eastern scholarship with one sweeping generality and spewing contempt for Oriental literary culture, Macaulay emphasized that the English language alone would bring light to the natives. He said, "Whether we look at the intrinsic value of our literature, or at the particular situation of this country, we should see the strongest reason to think that, of all foreign tongues, the English tongue is that which would be the most useful to our native subjects."[212] After denying any value in Oriental languages, law, culture, and religion, Macaulay

---

209. Minute of February 2, 1835, *Selections From Educational Records*, vol. 1, p. 116. Quoted in Thomas Metcalf, *The Aftermath of Revolution*, p. 22.
210. See Charles E. Trevelyan, *The Life and Letters of Lord Macaulay*, vol. 1, pp. 320-321.
211. H. Woodrow, ed., *Macaulay's Minutes on Education in India* (Calcutta, 1862), p. 107.
212. Ibid., pp. 108-109.

proposed to stop printing literature in Arabic and Sanskrit, and to close colleges teaching in vernacular. He even threatened to resign as Chairman of the Committee on Education if the Government would not adopt his program.[213]

As a consequence, William Bentinck ordered an end to the funding of all Oriental institutions and printing of native literature. The money thus made available was used to promote "a knowledge of English literature and science through the medium of the English language."[214] In the attack against Oriental education Macaulay was joined by Duff and Trevelyan. Duff hoped English education would create a chain reaction in religio-cultural spheres in India. He expressed his wish when he wrote, "Like the laws which silently but with resistless power, regulate the movements of the material universe, these educational operations, which are of the nature and force of moral laws, (sic) will proceed onwards till they terminate in effecting a universal change in the national mind of India."[215]

Trevelyan also jumped on the band wagon to support his brother-in-law Macaulay and to praise his ardent admirer Duff. Trevelyan envisioned that the introduction of English education would mysteriously transform converts. They would develop taste and style like their European masters and become enthusiastic supporters of the British Crown. He wrote, "Educated in the same way, interested in the same objects, engaged in the same pursuits with ourselves, they become more English than Hindus, just as the Roman provincials became more Roman than Gauls, or Italians."[216]

Furthermore, Trevelyan, expressing his view of what the people and country should be like as a result of English education, reveals his inward desire.

We want native functionaries of a new stamp, trained in a new school; and adding to the acuteness, patience, and intimate acquaintance with the language and manners of the people

213. Ibid., pp. 114-115.
214. Henry Herbert Dodwell, *The Cambridge History of the British Empire* (Cambridge: University Press, n.d.), vol. 5, p. 112.
215. See *Missionary Register* for 1836, p. 400; quoted in Bruce McCully, *English Education*, p. 70.
216. Charles Trevelyan, *Life and letters of Lord Macaulay*, p. 190.

which may always be expected in natives, some degree of the enlightened views and integrity which distinguish the European officers.[217]

Another illuminating point substantiating my argument that English education was introduced precisely to create a country of clerks and "half-breeds" is that Bengal government was directed by the Charter Act of 1813 to spend "a sum of one lakh of rupees" from the annual surplus for Western education. The resolution says, "(the money may be spent for) the revival and improvement of literature and the encouragement of the learned natives of India and for the introduction or promotion of a knowledge of the sciences among the inhabitants of the British territories in India."[218]

However, the Bengal government took ten years before the Governor-General appointed a Committee of Public Instruction. During this period the Indian Government was gravely concerned about loss of revenue forcing the local government "to reduce the cost of administration."[219] When the government learned that training and appointing natives would contribute to for cost-cutting and cheap labor, the administration joined the progressive thinkers, the private traders, and the British missionaries in supporting for the introduction of English education. C.H.Philips summarized the prevalent notion of government's interest in English education when he wrote, "For the home government the problem of education became closely knit with the problem of providing trained Indians for the government service."[220]

As a result, the Directors announced in Bengal Despatches, 5 September 1827 that the first object of improved education should be to prepare a body of individuals for discharging public duties. The public duties would include collecting taxes from the native population and maintaining the administrative machinery without disruption. Stanley summarizes the administrators' real motive behind this policy.

---

217. Ibid., pp. 158-159.
218. The Madras and Bombay Provinces were exempted from this clause, since they had to suffer annual deficits. See *The Cambridge History of India*, vol. 6., p. 104.
219. Cyril H. Philip, *The East India Company*, p. 247.
220. Ibid., 247. Also *The Cambridge History of India*, vol. 6, p. 109.

If revenue was to be raised from within the colonies by taxation, administrative machinery was required to collect it. The greater the revenue required, the more elaborate the machinery had to be, and the greater the risk of social unrest, necessitating higher expenditure on police and other mechanisms of control. In the long term, therefore, the effect of the constant pressure for immediate revenue was an escalation in both the risks and the cost of colonial rule. Financial stringency was the chief reason for the growing weight of British intervention in late nineteenth century India.[221]

The proposition was soon made a law and promoted the Western model of education which gave secondary status to the printing of books in Sanskrit, Persian, and Arabic and teaching in vernacular languages.

It was in this context that Duff and his colleagues joined with the administrators and spoke of the ontological advantages of English education, expressed their concern for material benefits of the government and developed a theory of missionary enterprise. Duff was beguiled by his fantasy of Western education's transcendence and the universality of its application. Obsessed by the superiority of Anglo-Saxon culture, and distracted by his limited understanding of Indian culture and faulty understanding of native religions, Duff collaborated with the colonizers to implement the educational system. In doing so, he cut himself off from the biblical understanding of Christian mission, the power of the cross, the dynamics of preaching the Gospel, the proper understanding of the people of India and the independence of mission without colonial accomplices.

Hence, in my view Duff's mission policy, in effect, was an updated repetition of sixteenth-century Jesuit and eighteenth-century Protestant missionaries' position, and was designed to perpetuate the colonial existential sentiments. To that effect, all colonial mission societies have some common traits: they were all internally consistent, externally connectable, and politically amenable to continuous extension. This mix of common characteristics and study of colonial mission values makes up nineteenth-century colonial missiography.

---

221. Brian Stanley, *The Bible and the Flag*, p. 49.

In summary, Duff's educational mission failed to produce an effective, evangelistic theology and a consistent, missiological theory that is premised on a biblical foundation which is "more equitable and non-coercive than a theory of fateful superiority." The notion of India as a cultural and spiritual wasteland served the mission purposes of Duff and his colleague, as much as it aided the colonizers. By associating India and its populace with a perverted spirituality and primitive backwardness, colonial mission in general has gained substantial European support. The roots of a theology of isolation and politics of prejudice lived not only in colonial ideology, but also in the logic of nineteenth-century Christian mission itself.

In this sense colonial mission went hand-in-hand with colonial ideology and Western aesthetic idioms. Hence, nineteenth-century mission, including its educational mission in India, was a structure formed in the core of an imperial context. Colonial mission worked within a dominant axiom to shape the style and content of missiography; there is no nineteenth-century mission policy, no evangelistic structure that has stood free of imperial, cultural, and political formations that give colonial mission its peculiar individuality.

CHAPTER VII

Colonial Mission and Colonial Epistemology: Dual Commitment

One of the striking developments of nineteenth-century British India after 1833 was the proliferation of mission societies, and the penetration of missionaries into the hitherto impregnable, orthodox Hindu communities across the nation. An important corollary of this trend has been the extension of British government from Cape Comorin to the Himalayas, and from Calcutta to Bombay, except for some small enclaves of the country that remained under French and Portuguese occupation. The Mutiny of 1857, the end of the East India Company, and the transfer of administrative power to the Crown also played important roles in the multiplication of mission societies.

Missionaries crisscrossed the country and established mission stations in all pockets of society. When a competition for converts and geographical areas arose, the societies formed an agreement among themselves under "comity" and divided their work area along geographical lines. Although comity became a viable means for applying missionary efforts to the effective evangelization of India, it created deep divisions along denominational and caste lines in the nineteenth century. In this chapter I would like to examine the exclusive domains of mission societies that were established across the nation, the impact of comity, and the intertwining of mission and colonialism during the second half of the nineteenth century.

In earlier chapters I argued that missionary work was done in the nineteenth century cannot be simply understood in terms of missionary evangelical outreach itself. It must be understood against the wider backdrop of British India's historical, political, and cultural conditions. My argument throughout has been that nineteenth-century missionary work cannot be separated from the macro-cosmic events that were articulated and exercised by means of colonial knowledge and power. What was distinctive about nineteenth-century mission was that it maintained the legacy and the residue of the anglicization of India.

The European mission Societies never strayed from one-dimensional understandings of colonized citizens in India. The Societies never went beyond the broad strokes of dominant European thinking about Indian people as inferior, superstitious, and eternally lost. The only way to redeem them was to civilize and convert them. For instance, the Report of the Secretary of State and Council of India upon the Moral and Material Progress and Condition of India in 1871-72 gave a detailed account of the work of missionary societies in India and its blessing to the people and the Empire. Along those lines, I already discussed in the last chapter how Duff, in his zeal for evangelizing the natives tried to introduce English education to civilize and missionize India, but overlooked provision for a vital mode of legitimization to enable the native converts to cope with the precariousness of social reality caused by the colonizers.

This created both theological and theoretical difficulties. Duff's strong belief in the transcendence of European civilization and in the universality of English education for evangelizing the people characterized Christian faith as a self- contained system of ideas devoid of social context. The rich and complex interplay of the political and missionizing processes in nineteenth-century India created an intellectualistic and deterministic approach to mission. As a result, a dynamic and existentially oriented mission, which I discuss in the following pages was introduced to combat the complexities of a colonized nation.

The Mutiny, the East India Company and the Crown

The legalization of English education, the abolition of restrictions on missionary presence, and the arrival of administrative leaders who were sympathetic to the evangelicals facilitated the proliferation of mission societies and Christian institutions across the nation. Scottish missionaries, such as John Wilson in Bombay (1832), John Anderson in Madras (1837), and Stephen Hislop in Nagpur (1844) established schools after the model of Duff to promote Christian knowledge among young native students. They were joined by the Church Missionary Society, the Baptist Missionary Society, the London Missionary Society, the Basel Mission, and others, in other parts of the nation. More American mission societies also entered India after 1833. The American Baptists sent their missionaries in 1835. They were followed by the American Lutherans and other societies in the 1840s.

However, the rapid growth of mission societies in India was halted by the Sepoy Mutiny in 1857 which was a violent reaction to British power. Mutinies had also broken out in earlier years.[222] But they were all confined to the regional level. The Mutiny of 1857 was so violent, and so explosive that its conflagration spread all across North India and consumed many Europeans on its way.

The Mutiny of 1857 was neither the outcome of fear nor of hatred toward Christianity, but of genuine misunderstanding by the British India government which had failed to take into account the religious and cultural sentiments of the people in India and the ruthless attitude of the British administrators in humiliating native leaders. The Mutiny was the last struggle of a nearly doomed Indian religious culture which channeled its anger through discontented sepoys. Even before 1857 there were sporadic outbursts against British authority. But the Mutiny of 1857 was the result of several accumulated grudges against the government.[223]

When regions such as Burma, Assam, Coorg, Sindh, the Punjab and Avadh were unjustly annexed, native kings and aristocracies were cast down and reduced to servitude; local craftsmen and artisans who worked for the aristocrats were deprived of their source of income.[224] The caste Hindus thought that their dearest symbols were destroyed and emptied of meaning. Since some of their sacred religious concepts were either being destroyed or distorted, the Hindus began to wonder whether they would ever be able to think religiously and live peacefully. To them it seemed certain that they would never again be able to establish their religious supremacy. As for the rest of the native kings, "The Doctrine of Lapse," introduced by Lord Dalhousie, sent tremors across the native kingdoms. [225]

---

222. Vellore mutiny 1806, Barrackpur 1824, Assam 1825, Sholapur, 1838, 1839 during the first Afghan war, disturbances in the Punjab in 1849, Govindgarh in 1850.

223. R.C. Majumdar, *British Parmountcy and Indian Renaissance*, pp. 435-459.

224. See Eugene Stock, *History of the Church Missionary Society*, vol. 2, p. 77.

225. The kingdoms of Nagpur, Satara, Jhansi and a number of minor territories were annexed to the British dominions by the policy of the Doctrine of Lapse introduced by Lord Dalhousie, the then Governor-General of India. The policy stated that a King would lose his kingdom, if he did not have male heirs.

Moreover, the native rulers were replaced by a judiciary and administrative machinery which was solely operated by the British. Native leaders were excluded from holding any responsible jobs in high-ranking positions. Over the years British-India administrative government became very arrogant and perfunctory. R.C.Majumdar summarizes how a police order issued in Agra, put down the native population.

Every native, whatever his pretended rank may be, ought to be compelled, under heavy penalties, to salaam [salute] all English gentlemen in the streets, and if the native is on a horse-back or in a carriage, to dismount and stand in a respectful attitude until the European has passed him.[226]

The order was issued with an intention to humiliate Indian people. Along with the disgraceful edict was ushered in the virtual presence of missionaries, who were openly sympathetic to Christianity as teachers in schools, as inspectors of schools, and, as magistrates in courts. The high caste communities were afraid that the newly introduced Christian religion would make them casteless. Their fear became real when both the caste and casteless people were asked to travel in the same train compartments and receive equal treatment in hospitals without caste distinction. To with those fears was added the greased cartridge which convinced both soldiers and natives that the government was determined to make them lose caste and embrace Christianity. This kind of social transformation evoked a drastic response: the Mutiny.

Fortunately, for the British, the uprising was limited almost entirely to North India. The military posts in Madras, Bombay, and the Punjab did not participate in the rebellion. With the help of troops from the Punjab and the South, the British contained the mutineers within a year and British authority was restored.[227] Politically and administratively, however, the uprising forced the

---

The adopted sons were not recognized as heirs. Further, Dalhousie abolished the titles of the Nawab of Carnatic and the Raja of Tanjore. He also stopped the pensions being paid by the administration to former Peshwa Baji Rao after his death. See R.C. Majumdar, *British Paramountcy and Indian Renaissance*, pp. 301, 406-408.

226. R.C. Majumdar, *British Paramountcy and India Renaissance*, p. 417.

227. Ibid., pp. 559-588.

British government to put an end to the existing East India
Company and its commercial enterprise, and to transfer the Indian
administrative Government to the Crown in 1858.[228]

The commercial control and political order that were regulated
and maintained by the Crown were not in any way different
from the administration of the East India Company. Both systems
maintained peace by force. The nation was forced to inherit the
colonizers' way of Government, law, and administration which
was basically asymmetrical. At one end stood Europeans endowed
with privileges, judged under a separate law and tried only in
the Supreme court at Calcutta which was made-up of all-white
Europeans; and at the other end stood the disinherited, the
colonized who were tried under a common law and were deprived
of their fundamental rights and freedom in their own country.
India was, at last, contained in 1858. Hope for freedom and
independence from European authority vanished.

Except for small regions in the SouthEast and the NorthWest,
all of India was either directly or indirectly under the Crown.
With meticulous care and minute detail, communication and
transportation systems were strengthened to connect the metro-
politan cities for quick mobilization of armed forces. Majumdar
holds that transportation and communication facilities were built
for an efficient administration and forceful control of the people.
Majumdar asserts:

> As per the Minute of 1853 Lord Dalhousie introduced railways
> in India "to immensely increase the striking power of his
> military forces at every point of the Indian Empire," to "bring
> British capital and enterprise to India," to "secure commerce
> and social advantages to India," and to "bring into the ports
> produce from the interior." [229]

Although the building of railways and roads did facilitate travel,
the construction of the railways did not aid in generating any industrial growth or agricultural production. In reality, they advanced
the British penetration of the Indian market by foreign goods
and tended to perpetuate the existing economic backwardness.

---

228. Eugene Stock, *History of the Church Missionary Society*, vol 2, pp. 220ff.
229. R.C. Majumdar, *British Paramountcy and India Renaissance*, pp. 384-385.

Stanley claims that, after the Mutiny of 1857 was silenced and India was brought directly under the Crown, British public funds flowed in millions into India to build railways and communication systems. The mission societies in Britain kept the public informed of the advantages of investing funds in India. The evangelical leaders asserted that transportation and communication systems in India would break down the segregation which happened to be the primary hindrance for the furtherance of the gospel and a chief curse to caste-ridden Indian society. The response from the people and business entrepreneurs in England was overwhelming. Stanley concludes:

A navigation scheme in central India undertaken in response to commercial pressure from Lancashire cotton interest became the means of establishing a new CMS mission on the Godaveri River in 1861. India experienced its own version of 'commerce and Christianity.'[230]

Foreign capital investment on these projects yielded enormous profit and interest. G.V.Joshi refers to this economic phenomenon ironically as an Indian subsidy to British interest. In a similar vein, N.V.Tilak compares the role of colonized monetrism to an act of "decorating another's wife."[231] Colonial economy aided; Britain bloomed.

In fact the railway and road systems helped the British open the Indian market to British manufactures, enabled the export of raw materials and foodstuffs, promoted the sale of British steel and machine products, and provided an opening for investment of surplus British capital, while facilitating the movement of the armed forces.[232] It looked as though India had gone under for ever. It had to wait for a whole generation for the resurrection of a nearly dead nationalistic movement which was to make the first half of the twentieth century eventful.

---

230. Brian Stanley, *The Bible and the Flag*, p. 103.
231. G.V. Josh, *Writings and Speeches* (Poona, India: 1912), p. 145.
232. Ibid.

British Colonization and its Effect Upon
Indian National Psyche

During the second half of the nineteenth century, British capital and investment began to flow into the country. Investing money on construction of railways and other industries became profitable. John Clark Marshman wrote in 1868: "Fifty nine thousand proprietors of stock and debentures have acquired a direct interest in the propriety of our Indian administration, and in the permanence of our rule."[233] In 1880, Richard Temple wrote that England should retain India perpetually. He states: "vast amount of British capital had been sunk in the country, on the assurance of British rule being, humanly speaking, perpetual."[234] The contracts for construction of railroads and other major undertakings were given to British entrepreneurs who made huge profits which they divided with their share holders.[235]

As much as Western historians romanticized the presence of the colonial government, their philanthropic motives, and their benevolent deeds, the East India Company had only one goal: commerce. The British India government had only one motive: rule. This colonial setting infused a fateful relationship of superiority and inferiority, master and slave, conqueror and conquered which conferred immense power on the colonizers to order and shape the country according to their whims and fancies for the pride of the Empire.[236] As early as 1829 the colonizers boasted,

> Whatever may be the fate of the several British colonies at some future and distant period, it is something at least to have spread our laws and language, and moral character, over the most distant parts of the globe.[237]

Since their sole purpose for being in India was to rule, to rule effectively, and to facilitate commerce, the British perpetuated a

---

233. *Quarterly Review*, July 1868, p. 48.
234. Richard Temple, *Indian in 1880*, 3rd ed. (London: J. Murray, 1881), p. 497.
235. R.C. Majumdar, *British Paramountcy and Indian Renaissance*, pp. 384ff, 856ff.
236. Goldwin Smith, *The Empire* (Oxford: J.H. & J. Parker, 1863). Preface, pp. viii-ix.
237. New Colony on Swan River, "Quarterly Review *39 (1829), quoted by Klaus E. Knorr in* British Colonial Theories, *p. 364.*

discourse about the need to colonize India. As early as 1833, with a predetermined mind, Macaulay said, "We are trying to give a good government to a people to whom we cannot give a free government."[238] Even deeds of Ellenborough, Dalhousie, and Lytton, much romanticized by mission historians, need only to be re-read from the colonized people's point of view.

Mission historians praise Marques of Dalhousie for his outstanding performance as a true Englishman in India and his contribution to Christian mission through his "conquest, consolidation and development."[239] Dalhousie was repeatedly lauded for his administrative policies, as they facilitated the furtherance of the missionary enterprise.[240] The missionaries' appreciation of the colonizers for their territorial expansion boosted their image in Britain's public mind.

Colonial history in India, whether it was under the East India Company or the Crown, was a shabby history of manipulation. The face of nineteenth-century India was lined with complex wrinkles which were created in the polluted atmosphere of economic exploitation and oppressive colonial administration. After the Crown took over, India underwent a full course of colonial modernization. Under the banner of modernization, economic development and transplantation of capitalism, India was transformed into a classic British colony. Once the traditional cotton and spinning industries were destroyed, no attempt was made by the British to revive and update them with the then modern technology which England was experiencing on the heels of the industrial revolution. Reviving and modernizing the spinning industry in India would pose an economic hazard to cotton mills in Lancashire. The colonizers modernized and upgraded mostly the courts and administrative systems, transportation and communication facilities, in order to make them effective tools for controlling the colonized masses.

The selective updating process shattered the economic and political cornerstone of the old Indian society. It dissolved the old

---

238. *Quoted in R.C. Majumdar, British Paramountcy and Indian Renaissance,* p. 319.
239. See William Wilson Hunter, *Rulers of India: Dalhousie* (Oxford: Clarendon Press, 1895), p. 11.
240. Eugene Stock, *History of the Church Missionary Society,* vol. 4, pp. 156-157.

pre-capital mode of production and generated a new colonial mode of operation. For example, the land tenure systems introduced after 1793 completely overturned the old agrarian relations. The agrarian structure that was originated to suit the needs of the colonizers (and under the impact of administrative and economic forces released by it) was new, and hence, it became semi-feudal. Throughout the Indian social structure, new relations and new classes were instituted to bolster the goals and objectives of the colonizers. The updated administrative processes produced monetary change without generating economic development. As a result, the budgetary gap between the 1800s and the 1900s got so wide that India became a classic underdeveloped nation of imitators and second-class workers, but not inventors or producers.

Indians who worked for the administration became part of the machinery steered decisively by the British. One of the pre-requisites in finding a job in that machinery was English knowledge. Clerks and English teachers gained new dignity. English schools, which were mostly run by mission societies, began to flourish. During this period no professional schools or centers for training apprenticeships were started.

With the oddity of English education and language in the field of employment, the conquered were forced to learn and communicate in their masters' language. Learning the English language became a way to secure employment. As a result, native culture, religions and traditions were pushed aside. The aged artisans and craftsmen were not able to learn the new language; neither were they taught any new tooling techniques and so they were forced to become agriculturists. Those newly made agriculturists moved into rural areas to join their farming cousins, making India look like a nation of farmers. Further, the superiority of the British-induced in the mind through English education, communication, transportation and a strong administration created a sense of inferiority, dependence, and a belief in the inevitability of British rule. This interiorized belief in European superiority was perpetuated by colonial institutions as well. As a result, the colonizers had to use less and less force to maintain peace and order as the close of the century drew near.

This dual cultural climate, created by English education and bilingual communication established by the administration made an adverse impact on the national psyche. Those who were able to learn English began to feel the psychological and emotional burden of what Albert Memmi calls "linguistic dualism."[241] In his book *The Colonizer and the Colonized,* Memmi aptly summarizes the struggle of the colonized who had to learn their masters' language in order to find a job.

The difference between native language and cultural language is not peculiar to the colonized, but colonial bilingualism cannot be compared to just any linguistic dualism. Possession of two languages is not merely a matter of having two tools, but actually a means of participation in two psychical and cultural realms. Here, the two worlds symbolized and conveyed by the two tongues are in conflict; they are those of the colonizer and the colonized. Furthermore, the colonized's mother tongue, that which is sustained by his feelings, emotions, and dreams, that in which his tenderness and wonder are expressed, thus that which holds the greatest emotional impact, is precisely the one which is the least valued. It has no stature in the country or in the concert of peoples. If he wants to obtain a job, make a place for himself, exist in the community and the world, he must first bow to the language of his masters. In the linguistic conflict within the colonized, his mother tongue is that which is crushed. He himself sets about discarding this infirm language, holding it from the sight of strangers. In short, colonial bilingualism is neither a purely bilingual situation in which an indigenous tongue coexists with a purists language . . . nor a simple polyglot richness benefitting from an extra but relatively neuter alphabet, it is a linguistic drama.[242]

This linguistic drama in India was enacted in the cultural and social theater of English-speaking Indians. As performers in the drama struggled to combine both traditional, cultural elements and liberal, intellectual strides introduced by English education, they began to experience conflicting emotional pain and disturbing social and cultural agony which no European ever attempted to understand.

---

241. Albert Memmi, *The Colonizer and the Colonized* trans. Howard Greenfield (New York: Orion Press, 1965), p. 106.
242. Ibid., pp. 107-108.

The Sepoy Mutiny and Mission's Interiorization

As I explained earlier, the Mutiny was not an anti-missionary movement. It was the result of the frustration of the sepoys who were poorly paid and who were never promoted above the ranks of British soldiers, and the lack of trust in the British-India government. The uprising was not aimed against Christian missionaries or Christian religion itself. Although several missionaries in north India were killed, they were murdered mainly because they belonged to the country where the colonizers came from. After the mutiny was contained, missionaries who were working in other parts of the country gathered data to prove that the uprising had never occurred in places where mission stations had been established and converts won.[243] Hence missionaries and their societies resolved to intensify their evangelistic work, and asked the government to aid the mission societies in their evangelistic endeavor.

The missionaries' goal was to gain more converts and earn the confidence of the native population so as to permanently establish the British Raj in India. T.S. Burnell, in his letter to the *Gazette and Courier* written 15 June 1857 from Malur, Madura, defended British rule in India, expressed his concern for Christian mission, and fostered the pride and prestige of British people.

> How earnestly should we desire and pray for the spread of Christianity in this country. The one and only bond of unity which is ever likely to bind India to England is common Christianity. Our religion is now the source of disunion; but when the truth shall have set the native mind free and when he who was a murderer from the beginning shall have lost his hold upon the millions of India, then England, if permitted to be the honoured instrument of God's grace, will reign in the affections of an emancipated and happy people. [244]

In the letter he also mentioned what was to be done to restore the power and pride of Britain in India.

---

243. See K.S. Latourette, *History of the Expansion of Christianity,* vol. 6, pp. 131-132.

244. Quoted in M.M. Kuriakose, *History of Christianity in India: Source Materials* (The Christian Literature Society: Madras, 1982), pp. 168-169.

We hope that the rebellion will soon be put down, and present peace be restored, but confidence cannot possibly return, nor will there exist any security, until the constitution of the Bengal native army has been thoroughly remodelled. The Brahmins must be eliminated; the sepoys must be brought into subjection. After all, the British Government will suffer more from loss of prestige throughout Asia, and especially in the eyes of our native subjects, than from any other cause. It will take many years to restore this under most favourable circumstances, and the progress of events does not lead us to suppose that circumstances will be very favourable to the re-establishment of British power and pride.[245]

Missionaries in India and the evangelicals in England, citing the cause of the Mutiny and pointing out the geographical location where it occurred, demanded that the government commit itself to the propagation of Christianity.[246] In England the Evangelicals sided with the missionaries and maintained that the Mutiny did not occur in places where missionaries and converts were present. Evangelizing India would make Indians loyal to the Crown.[247] The Prime Minister, Lord Palmerston, and a few other British officials were in favor of the promotion of Christianity. Two years after the Mutiny, in a public address, Lord Palmerston stated:

It is not only our duty, but in our own interest, to promote the diffusion of Christianity as far as possible throughout the length and breadth of India.[248]

He was supported by the Secretary of State, Sir Charleswood, when he said, "every additional Christian is an additional bond of union with this country and an additional source of strength to the Empire."[249] But the Queen, while confessing her own faith and the faith of the British nation, disclaimed the imposition of her faith on Indian people and proclaimed toleration of religious beliefs. She declared,

245. Ibid., p. 169.
246. Eugene Stock, *History of the Church Missionary Society,* vol. 2, p. 236.
247. Ibid., pp 232-35.
248. Arthur Mayhew, *Christianity and the Government of India,* p. 194.
249. Ibid., p. 194.

Firmly relying ourselves on the truth of Christianity and acknowledging with gratitude the solace of religion, we disclaim alike the right and the desire to impose our convictions on any of our subjects. We declare it to be our Royal pleasure,that none be in any wise favoured, none molested or disquieted by reason of their religious law; and we do strictly charge and enjoin those who may be in authority under us that they abstain from all interference with the religious belief or worship of any of our subjects, on pain of our highest pleasure.[250]

In spite of the government's policy of neutrality, individual government officers did provide mission societies with money and other necessities. Besides, forceful political environment, strong military presence, and imperial administrative policies created a very favorable climate for mission societies to thrive. Sir Charles Aitchison, commenting on the inconsistency of the policy of neutrality, said that the policy, in effect, did not deter government officials from promoting Christianity in India.

Looked at in the light of the practice of the present day, when officers of every degree take part in missionary meetings, and the highest in India, not omitting the Viceroy himself lay the foundation-stones of mission schools and churches, and acknowledge from the public platform the indebtedness of the Government to the Christian missionary.[251]

As a result, more and more new societies began to arrive in India. Firth enumerates,

The Methodist Episcopal Church of America, the University Missions, the English, Irish and Canadian Presbyterians, the Canadian Baptists, the Society of St.John the Evangelist, and others; old Societies such as the C.M.S. and the W.M.M.S., extended their work into new areas; till hardly any part of the country was without a Christian mission somewhere at work in it.[252]

---

250. John W. Kaye, *Christianity in India: An Historical Narrative,* (London: Smith Elder & Co., 1859), p. 496.
251. Quoted in Eugene Stock, *History of the Church Missionary Society,* vol. 2, p. 261.
252. Cyril Firth, *Introduction to Indian Church History,* p. 184.

As mission societies began to work in different parts of the country, they began to feel the need to "join forces and pool their forms of church government and of worship."[253] As a result, regional mission conferences were held in Calcutta (1855), Benares (1857), and Ootacamund (1858) in order to cover the Bengal, NorthWest, and South India Provinces. Having experienced some success with regional conferences, the first major General Missionary Conference for the whole of India was arranged in 1872 in Allahabad where 132 missionaries participated. Two major items on the agenda were to join missionary forces together in order to have a common form of worship and church government and to maintain cordial relationships between missionaries and converts. Educated Indian Christian leaders and outstanding missionaries such as Jacob Chamberlain of the Arcot Mission of The Reformed Church in America appealed to their colleagues to organize a one, united "Church of Christ in India." Their request was denied, and the union never did take place. Relations between missionaries and converts never got any better. The Conferences brought only a collection of mission societies together, but not a collectivity of thought and theology.

The Conference held in 1879 at Bangalore emphasized the necessity of unity and oneness among Christian mission agencies in India. They were able to come together to discuss methods of evangelism and forms of worship but not to address the issue of unity. C.C.Fenn, the Secretary of the C.M.S., read a paper at the Centenary Missionary Conference in London in 1888 emphasizing Missionary Comity and called for the Mission Societies to recognize each other as members of one body, the Church of Christ.[254] Native Christians began to demand Christian unity. They claimed that the existing division among Indian converts was scandalous and it was created by missionaries themselves. Christian communities are sundered by the mere "accident of having been baptized in one of the Sectarian Churches," which happened to be in their geographical location.[255]

---

253. Bengt Sundkler, *Church of South India: The Movement Towards Union 1900-1947* (London: Lutterworth Press, 1954), p. 24.
254. See Eugene Stock, *Report of the Missionary Conference of the Anglican Communion* (1894), p. 178.
255. *A Collection of Papers Connected with the Movement of the National Church of India* (Madras, 1893), p. 144.

It was during this time that the Indian National Congress was founded, which gave a renewed impetus to the demands of Indian Christians for one united church and mission society. Strong proponents from the Indian side were Dr.Pulney Andy, J.P.Cotelingam, and Prof. S.Satianadhan. A few missionaries, such as T.M.Scott of Madura, also supported this idea.

One distinctive characteristic of nineteenth-century mission was that it maintained the legacy and the residue of the Europeanization of India. Mission conferences were preoccupied with one theme: win more converts in order to establish the church permanently. It could be done only if mission societies maintained their individual identity. Despite repeated pleas from national Christian leaders for one united church, no serious effort was taken to come together as one united mission church or to formulate an ecumenical theology. Furthermore, the missionaries were so inexperienced in working in a cross-cultural context that they never considered the necessity to contextualize the Gospel and the need to confess Christ relevantly in a pluralistic society. In short, they never took interest in developing a coherent and carefully developed biblical theology of mission for the non-Western cultural, religious, and polycrat society.

One of the prerequisites for unity is the understanding of local culture, language and philosophy in which the church has been located. The European analytical approach to Indian philosophy and systematic approach to theology led missionaries to the conclusion that one particular form of Protestant theology (European Protestant evangelical theology) was absolute and therefore, authoritative. Underlying this approach was the idea of missiological ethnocentrism.[256]

In addition, mission societies failed to develop a social analysis that would enable them to understand the mechanics of injustice and exploitation caused by the colonizers. The missionaries not only had an inadequate understanding of human rights and human justice for the colonized, but made a virtue out of colonization by supporting it. After all, it was the colonial government that enabled them to carry out missionary work in India.

---

256. See Daniel J. Adams, *Cross-Cultural Theology* (Atlanta: John Knox Press, 1987), pp. 63-72.

None of the mission conferences held in the nineteenth century condemned the evils caused by colonialism. Missionaries who preached sin and salvation, forgiveness and reconciliation to their native converts ignored preaching to their own countrymen of the message of Christian love, the meaning of reconciliation, the theology of restitution and the biblical principles of justice. In this respect missionary spirituality stumbled in manifesting itself in the form of insight, discernment and understanding. All that the societies were able to do was medical and educational relief work here and there or wherever the converts were present.

Although relief mission, which I would call "the ambulance ministry,[257] "was a genuine attempt to alleviate the sufferings of native people, it did not relieve the Indian people from cruel sufferings inflicted by the colonizers. Further, mission societies were not too interested in the existential and political sufferings of the people. Because the societies were interested primarily in saving the souls of "heathens" and gaining converts, the missionaries tended to treat Christianity as an otherworldly affair which did not have much to do with the affairs of the present world. Over the years the societies' methodological substructure was characterized by a degree of obscurity and their hermeneutics soon became the hermeneutics of the colonizers.

On the other hand, some enlightened colonizers, who had wanted to hold India by its affection, openly condemned the evils caused by the British.[258] As early in 1843, Richard Cobden expressed his feelings about British rule in India when he said,

The system upon which our colonial affairs were now conducted was one of unmixed evil, injustice, and loss to the people of this country."[259]

He saw British rule in India "with an eye of despair" and found it "a calamity and a curse."[260] That sentiment was shared by John Bright and Goldwin Smith when they opposed the

---

257. See *Kairos Document.*
258. See Bright and J.E.T. Rogers (eds.,), *Speeches on Question of Public Policy by Richard Cobden,* (London, 1870), vol. 1, p. 485.
259. Quoted in Klaus Knorr, *British Colonial Theories,* p. 373.
260. John Morley, *The Life of Richard Cobden,* new ed. (London: Chapman and Ball Limited, 1883), p. 532.

colonization of India as an unmitigated evil and tyranny.[261] All
of them called for England to make restitution. John Bright
announced,

> [The Indian people] whom you have subdued, and who have
> the highest and strongest claims upon you—claims which you
> cannot forget—claims which, if you do not act upon, you may
> rely upon, if there be a judgement for nations . . . our children
> in no distant generation must pay the penalty which we have
> purchased by neglecting our duty to the populations of India.[262]

Even if the societies had not strengthened their positions to
ask for England to make restitution, they certainly could have
demanded that the colonizers to be fair and humane; just and
considerate to the powerless and colonized. By refusing to make
an investigation of the colonial exploitation and by moving along
with the political subjugation of the colonized, the mission societies
became "worldly" and opportunistic. Since their pro-colonial
missiology was predicated upon its commitment to the perpetuation
of European colonialism, and envisaging the goal of winning
converts as a means to an extraneous end, the nineteenth- century
colonial missiology became a political philosophy by carrying out
mission in a way that was consistent with colonial empiricism.
By submitting themselves to a form of cognitive self-limitation
and seeing the Indian people only as "human materials" to be
added into the fold and to build an ecclesiastical outer-structure,
the mission societies became epistemologically myopic. By doing
so, colonial missiology was neither in continuity with the mission
of the apostles nor in accord with an authentic imitation of the
praxis of the Jesus of the Gospels.

For example, the praxis of Jesus of Nazareth was the preaching
of the Kingdom of God and embodying it in his own actions on
behalf of the oppressed, the exploited, the poor, the needy, and
the suffering. It called for imitation in the praxis of his disciples.
After the death and resurrection of Jesus, his followers gathered
to form a koinonia community to continue his praxis which was
called the Church. The mission of the Church was to tell the

---

261. Goldwin Smith, *The Empire,* p. 145.
262. Ibid., p. 8.

story of the just God, the redemption of the whole person available in the person of Jesus Christ, and to imitate his praxis. The Church is a community which is premised upon a promise, and speaks to and about the world "in present time from a point beyond present time," as Richard John Neuhaus says.[263] Since the Church is in the world, and also speaks from *within* the world, the Church should address the needs of the koinonia community living in the world. Hence, the mission of the Church is prophetic; it penetrates into all spheres of human existence, and encompasses everything that happens in the community and the world.

In true biblical sense, nineteenth-century mission societies deviated from their theology of mission by interiorizing the exterior, and by developing a colonial epistemology which was a theological discourse of power and politics. This theology of power and politics has been aptly summarized by Charles Long in another context.

Theologies are about power, the power of God but equally about the power of the specific form of discourse about power.[264]

Theology, an effort at interpreting God's power, is also a human instrument, vulnerable enough to imbibe the existing hegemonic order; and a complex vehicle which conveys at once God's power through an hierarchized human power structure. That was why colonial mission was able to justify and work with a power structure that had subjected the whole subcontinent by force of arms and violence and assigned the people of the continent to the category of a "functional otherness."[265]

---

263. Richard John Neuhaus, *The Catholic Moment: The Paradox of the Church in the Postmodern World* (San Francisco: Harper and Row, 1987), p. 8.
264. Charles Long, "Freedom, Otherness and Religion: Theologies Opaque," in *The Chicago Theological Seminary Register* (Winter 1983): p. 20.
265. Ibid.

CHAPTER VIII

Comity and Colonial Mission

In this chapter I briefly analyze the theoretical effects of comity upon the cultural and social life of the Indian church and her members. Since the meaning of a text can be found, as Claude Geffre says, only in the "structures of text and the mechanics of its functioning," comity and its principles should be set in their functioning position and considered into from the colonized converts' point of view.[266]

Comity, in broad terms, means cooperation of mission societies on mission fields, the elimination of waste by overlapping of work and competition for converts, the division of geographical territory for effective evangelization of non-Christians, non-interference with one another's mission project, and respect for each other's missionary endeavor. The term comity won general acceptance only after the gathering of the Centenary Conference of Protestant Missions of the World at London in 1888.[267] By the beginning of the twentieth century, comity became an accepted policy of missionary work around the world and laid the foundation for the ecumenical movement. After World War I it began to lose its significance. In India comity began to lose its significance beginning in 1919, when the church union negotiation resumed.

European evangelical awakening and colonial expansion enlarged the vision of the church in the West in evangelizing "the heathens in far off lands." The Dutch East Indies Company and the English East India Company in foreign lands invited the presence of chaplains and facilitated the arrival of missionaries from Europe. The continual flow of Protestant missionaries in the middle of the nineteenth century demanded an organized nature of work to win converts for the church. European church and mission societies, for the first time, were faced with a challenge to do a new kind of mission to the peoples of non-European

---

266. Claude Geffre, *The Risk of Interpretation: On Being to the Christian Tradition in a Non-Christian Age,* trans. David Smith, (New York: Paulist Press, 1987), p. 14.
267. James Johnson, ed., *Report of the Centenary Conference on the Protestant Missions of the World, Held in Exeter Hall* (London: James Nisbet, 1888), vol. 2, pp. 429-62.

culture and religions. During the second half of the nineteenth century, the challenges and demands of the mission field brought all mission societies together for "effective occupation" and to offer support to each other in their enterprise. As a result, the SPCK, the SPG, the LMS, the CMS, the BMS, and the Basel Missionary Society helped one another through funding and personnel in order to establish the church in foreign lands. Commenting on the ecumenical cooperation and ecclesiastical unity that came out of comity, R. Pierce Beaver wrote,

> The C.M.S. and the L.M.S. employed German, Swiss, and Swedes, both Lutheran and Reformed Janicke's seminary in Germany supplied men for British and Dutch societies. The Basel Missionary Society (1815) united in a common venture Lutherans and Reformed in Switzerland and Germany, as did the Evangelical Missionary Society of Paris in France. Basel not only sent its people directly, but supplied missionaries for the C.M.S. and L.M.S. and pastors for Reformed, Lutheran and Evangelical churches in the United States . . . Every Missionary society published news about the activities of the others in the magazine. These accounts were read in the Monthly Concert of Prayer for Missions. Thus the early participants in the Protestant Missionary enterprise were drawn together, influenced each other, supported each other, and felt a sense of unity and brotherhood not known to the other clergy and laity in the churches in a time of denominational isolation. The very battle against indifference, inertia, and official oppositions which they had to wage for recognition of the missionary privilege and obligation sharpened their sense of unity and common purpose.[268]

This sense of unity and common purpose was echoed in all the missionary conferences held in the nineteenth century. The Union Missionary Conference held in New York in 1854,[269] the London Missionary Conference,[270] and the Conference on Missions

268. R. Pierce Beaver, *Ecumenical Beginnings in Protestant World Mission---A History of Comity* (New York: Thomas Nelson & Sons, 1962), pp. 21, 22.
269. See *Proceedings of the Union Missionary Convention, Held in New York, May 4th and 5th, 1854* (New York: Taylor and Hogg, 1854), pp. 8-22.
270. "The Missionary Conference, Londs." Report by T.R. Brooke in *Evangelical Christendom* 3 (1854): pp. 432-33.

Held at Liverpool in 1860[271] went a step further and sought Christian unity both at home and abroad. In the Mission Conference held at New York in 1854, the special speaker was Alexander Duff himself. Duff proposed a resolution which was unanimously adopted.

> Resolved, That considering the vast extent of the yet unevangelized world of Heathenism, and the limited means of evangelization at the disposal of the existing evangelical Churches or Societies, it would be very desirable, that, with the exception of great centres, such as the capitals of powerful kingdoms, any efficient pre-occupancy of any particular portion of the Heathen field by any Evangelical Church or Society should be respected by others, and left in their undisturbed possession: At the same time acknowledging with thankfulness to God, that heretofore there has been so little interference with each other's fields of labour.[272]

In the spirit of unity, the Conference on Missions at Liverpool passed a resolution that

> Though belonging to different sections of the Church of Christ, they rejoice in that close union to each other and that practical cooperation which have so largely prevailed among the agents of Missionary Societies, both at home and abroad.[273]

Although most of the societies working in colonies recognized one another's validity, some high church societies such as the S.P.G continued to remain aloof. The Roman Catholic church and the Orthodox churches were never included in comity agreements. The societies that decided to recognize each other's ministry resolved to use their limited missionary resources for the effective evangelization of the territories without waste of time, money, or personnel; [274] hence they resolved to organize a

---

271. *Conference on Missions Held in 1860 at Liverpool* (London: Nisbet, 1860), pp. 10ff.
272. *Proceedings of the Union Missionary Convention* (New York, 1854), pp. 16-17.
273. *Conference on Missions Held in 1860 at Liverpool*, p. 12.
274. N.G. Clark, *Missionary Comity— Methods and Means for Carrying forward*

united publishing and distributing place, a center for training pastors and evangelists, and a joint organization for medical and education missions. This fraternal relationship was appreciated by the societies and fostered by missionaries. Comity elevated missionary work to a different but higher plane previously unknown either in the West or in the East. Beaver praises the harmony comity has offered

> Comity had been earlier the stepping stone to genuine mutuality and fellowship, it had then become the guarantee of non-interference in one another's affairs, but now it was looked upon as the by-product of genuine cooperation.[275]

This kind of missionary work paved the way for the organization of the World Missionary Conference at Edinburgh in 1910, the composition of the International Missionary Council, and the establishment of the National Council of Churches in the first quarter of the twentieth century. In the twentieth century comity was absorbed into the very cardiovascular system of Protestant missions and concern was expressed about movement toward organic union among the newly established churches in European colonies.[276]

Comity was discussed in India at the South India Missionary Conference held at Ootacamund in 1858, in which G.V.Pope of the S.P.G. presented a paper on comity. He outlined four fundamental factors which were essential for successful missionary work in India, and twelve laws that should govern missionaries and their societies in dealing with native converts and fellow workers. Pope's recommendations were accepted by the Conference, "to promote the true prosperity of the Native churches."[277]

However, comity was severely opposed by Bishop James Mills Thoburn of the American Methodist Episcopal Church at the

---

the Work in the Foreign Field, (Boston: American Board of Commissioners for Foreign Missions, 1886), pp. 1ff. Also H.P. Van Dusen, *One Great Ground of Hope—Christian Mission and Christian Unity* (Philadelphia: Westminster Press, 1961), pp. 17ff.

275. R. Pierce Beaver, *Ecumenical Beginnings,* p. 87.

276. I discuss this at length in the following chapter.

277. *Proceedings of the South India Missionary Conference Held at Ootacumund, April 19th-May 5th, 1858* (Madras: S.P.C.K., 1858), p. 337.

National Missionary Conference held at Allahabad from December 26, 1872 to January 1, 1875. He did not agree with the division of territory, and called for "working together in amity" and disciplining a mission society if one of its workers violated the principle of cooperation. He was contradicted by the Anglican Bishop Clifford of Lucknow and the conference voted not to pass any legislation. Eventually, at the South India Conference at Madras in 1900 and the Fourth Decennial Missionary Conference at Madras in 1902, comity was agreed upon and the Board of Arbitration was created.[278] It created a new kind of cooperation among mission societies, acceptance of each other's ministry and recognition of one another as the body of Christ on Indian soil.

Comity called attention to what could be done within colonized nations. It involved European missionary values. In principle it became a forerunner of the ecumenical movement and a challenge to church union in India. It established models of united effort, often while challenging societies to search for ways to connect together in foreign lands. Comity also played a role in institutionalizing mission societies and provided examples of what Christian missionary ideals could be while serving as a stimulus for the creation of a global missionary movement.

Although comity proved useful as a means of bringing missionaries of all denominations together for a common purpose, in practice it divided the converts on parochial, denominational and geographical lines. The twelve laws of comity proposed by Pope, which the conference adopted, adversely affected the Indian converts. Comity fostered a sense of suspicion against Christian converts and strangled the free movement of Christians in their own country. For instance, one of the rules stipulates that the missionaries should be wary and skeptical when a convert wishes to change his/her denominational affiliation. One of the stipulations of comity is not to admit any convert from another denomination without the consent of the convert's missionary. If any dispute should arise, the missionary alone should act as a mediator, not the local leader or the catechist.

Comity engendered an atmosphere of master/slave relationship in mission stations and empowered the missionaries to control

---

278. *Report of the Fourth Decennial Missionary Conference Held in Madras, December 11-18, 1902* (Madras: Christian Literature Service, 1903), pp. 160-64.

and manage the converts more effectively. The converts became the personal property of a denomination, numerical figures in their ledgers, and token pieces of the success of a mission society which worked in a particular geographical region. Comity did not allow the mission societies to take seriously the potential for native leadership.

Although it produced effective missionary leadership, comity failed to prepare the missionary for a servant role in the field setting. Since missionaries alone had to decide when, or if, a Christian community possessed the maturity to govern its own affairs—or when, or if, it should become autonomous—the native converts had to wait and look expectantly for their missionary master's final declaration.

Comity was created mainly for use in colonized nations by the societies which came from colonizing countries. It fostered a homogeneous unity among European Protestant societies. Like any other cultural and legal production of British India, comity was not an innocent selection of the best that had been thought and planned; rather, it was the institutionalization of those particular hegemonic mission artifacts that appeared best to convey and sustain the dominant social order. In that process it deliberately excluded the natives from participation in ecclesiastical order.

Comity was practiced as a magisterial privilege of the missionary societies. Like all other colonial decisions, comity was context-dependent and shaped by the structure of interest that sustained the "spiritual" transactions between missionaries and converts. For this reason comity should be interpreted in light of the political and cultural backdrop of nineteenth-century colonized India. Viewed against that background, as comity's rules and theories attest, even mission societies judged the converts in terms of European value judgements and institutional norms that they certified.

The practical ideas about the workings of comity were rarely derived from explicit theoretical principles of Christian mission or empirical encounters within a range of scriptures; rather, they were developed within the cultural frameworks that were in part constituted by notions of colonialism and European Protestant civilization. This became apparent when the societies tried to imagine how they could respond to someone coming from Europe but whose country had no colony in India (for example, Leipzig mission). Within these competing positions, comity served their self-interests and some of their psychological concepts.

The two basic aspects of self-interest were the desire for power over the native converts and the establishment of the church on a European model. Out of those aspects, comity's rules, principles, and ideologies were generated and sustained. But this is hardly an exhaustive account of needs, motives, and powers. My thesis is that at least three other claims seem possible, each with important consequences for the understanding of comity: missionary's positional superiority, evangelicals' otherworldly spirituality, and colonizers' structural exteriority.

Since comity began from within the "externals" of colonialism, it reinforced the spirit and pragmatic principles of European colonialism. For example, missionaries from some denominations and countries concentrated their work in particular provinces, among certain caste groups. Invariably, this meant that German missionaries were isolated in one part of a mission land, British in another, Americans in yet another, and so on. Hence, the small German church, English church, and American church each began to emerge with its own respective denominational traits. Since each missionary group thought that its cultural and religious traditions were superior to other forms of expression, and there was no outside challenge to such an assumption, churches were established after European models. The lack of ecumenical missiology and the undeveloped indigenous forms of religious life perpetuated the displanted church organization.

Finally, comity promoted effective evangelization of the people. It used a criteria that was existential in principle. The criteria restricted the freedom and movement of the converted natives. Comity's unity, meaning, and structure, which fascinated the mission leaders, failed to impress Indian Christians. After all, comity was concerned only about the souls of the converts, but not about the "whole and entire, body and soul."[279]

Comity never discussed the daily exchange between the religious and cultural life of the natives. Although it is presumptuous to expect nineteenth-century mission societies to develop an advanced theological and missiological understanding of culture and society, it is not unrealistic to expect them to develop biblical insights

---

279. *Gaudium et Spes*, par. 3.

into how the Gospel had to be preached through a process of exchange and dialogue with the people being evangelized. This exchange process, which is now called inculturation, not only gives but also receives insights about the people, culture and thoughts.[280] As a result, the church will care for the total human being and the search for justice becomes a constituent part of the mission of the church.

In spite of all its developments and plans, comity never allowed room for the development of vigorous support for the rights of the converts in regard to their national and cultural identity. Since the theology of the colonial mission remained undeveloped, it was difficult to explore fully the pastoral implications of the relationship between the missionary and his converts.

Since Europe and America had an endless supply of missionaries, and with the arrival of able colonial administrators such as Lawrence, Curzon, and others, there was no urgency to discover and accommodate Christian faith to local cultures and incorporate native leadership. As a result, mission societies continued to become dramatically *inter*national, but rarely did they become *supra*national.

---

280. See G. Arbuckle, "Inculturation, Community and Conversion," *Review for Religions* (Nov./Dec. 1985): pp. 847 ff.

CHAPTER IX

Nineteenth-Century Mission Theology and Indian Christian Identity

In this chapter I bring out the unequal relationship that existed between the native Christians and the missionaries, how it was voiced by V.S.Azariah at the Edinburgh Conference in 1910, and the subsequent demand for a national, independent church in India. I believe that the dominant European colonial structure, in the form of imperialism, influenced colonial mission in the production of scholarship, the organization of mission conferences, and the formation of a theology of mission. Hence, I attempt to interpret colonial missiology as a dynamic exchange between the missionaries and the larger political concern shaped by the colonizers within whose intellectual boundaries the ideas were conceived and brought forth.

Historical Background

The last decades of the nineteenth century and the first decade of the twentieth century were the heyday of the British administration and missionary expansion in India. The unity of the subcontinent became a reality. Law and order prevailed as they had not done for centuries. Politically, all rivalries were put down. Trade monopoly was permanently established. Travel became safe and easy. The scars of the Mutiny of 1857 were healed. The nationalistic movements were made nearly impotent. Inter-European rivalry on Indian soil was ended, and the Indian nation could be treated with such *propriete hauteur*.[281]

The mission societies were well established in India by the end of the nineteenth century. The societies began to gain more converts through mass movements among those classes that suffered most from the existing social and economic order.[282]

---

281. See D.K. Fieldhouse, *The Colonial Empire: A Comparative Survey from the Eighteenth Century* (New York: Delacorte Press, 1967), p. 178.
282. See K. S. Latourette, *A History of the Expansion of Christianity*, vol. 4, pp. 65-214. Also J. Waskom Pickett, *Christian Mass Movements in India* (Cincinnati: The Abingdon Press, 1933).

More and more missionaries, both single and married, began to arrive. For instance, CMS alone recruited 315 female missionaries for its overseas missions between 1890-99. The following chart taken from *The Bible and the Flag*, shows the swift increase in missionary recruits, both male and female, in the last decade of the nineteenth century.

Decennial totals of CMS recruits and candidates from Great Britain and Ireland, 1800-1900

Decade	All Recruits	Female Recruits	Male Recruits	Male Candidates not known
1800–09	2	0	2	
1810–19	28	0	28	
1820–29	80	7	73	
1830–39	104	7	97	
1840–49	76	9	67	
1850–59	133	5	128	561(+)
1860–69	132	6	126	518
1870–79	166	6	160	593
1880–89	250	0	210	606
1890–99	671	315	356	870

Note: Missionary wives are excluded. The figure for male candidates in the 1850s is marginally too low, since it excludes the first three months of 1850, for which no data are available.[283]

In Europe the evangelical awakening created interest in studying the Bible and its setting. The study of Eastern languages, culture, race, and literature was introduced in the European academia by the end of the nineteenth century. The continuing European expansion and exploration in the East placed Europe in a privileged and powerful position. When the religious awakening touched the academic campus, and the Student Volunteer Movement was formed with a motto to "evangelize the world in this generation," the first place that they could think of being present and doing missionary work was the colonized lands, particularly India.

---

283. Brian Stanley, *The Bible and the Flag*, p. 80.

At the end of the nineteenth century, India was further opened to Europe, to a large degree, as the result of continuing expansion of European exploration. The increasing influence of the Orientalists' publications, missionaries' reports, travel literature, commercial enterprises, colonial governments, and so on, brought India under more anatomical study. The prevailing opinion held in Europe was that India was degenerate, that its culture and religions were "the beastly devices of the heathen,"[284] and that only European religion and civilization could redeem them. As a result, a more focused and highly specialized form of evangelization was designed. In order to discuss more effective method of evangelism.in non-European countries and to foster unity and cooperation with fellow European Protestant missionaries, the Edinburgh Conference was organized in 1910.

In that process, the South American, Roman Catholic nations were left out. A careful reader might note that when Edinburgh talked about evangelizing the world, they actually meant Protestant Europe's colonized lands. By virtue of the positional superiority of the European missionaries and the presence of their fellow nationals as rulers in colonized lands, the missionaries' presence could be assured. Further, by the year 1914, 85 percent of the world was under European colonization, and the European could freely travel to establish his mission base anywhere in colonized lands without hindrance.[285]

Edinburgh's concept of mission was largely world evangelization and conversion of non-Christians. Thus it absolutely separated itself from the colonized people's struggle for independence and freedom. Freedom and liberation were preached and interpreted in a non-traditional way at the Conference. Those concepts were spiritualized, Christianized and structuralized. In his opening address at Edinburgh, Lord Balfour said,

By common consent there is just now a great opportunity. Nations in the East are awakening. They are looking for two

---

284. Michael Hollis, *Paternalism And `The Church* (London: Oxford University Press, 1962), p. 41.

285. An observation could be made here: All the majorconferences, Edinburgh 1910, Jerusalem 1928,Tambaram 1938—were held in the colonized zones; the conferences were planned, convened and dominated by the European missiologists and theologians.

things; they are looking for enlightenment and for liberty. Christianity alone of all religions meets these demands in the highest degree.[286]

Enlightenment and liberty were understood and interpreted from a spiritual point of view: the enlightening of minds from darkness and the liberation of natives from their bondage to superstition with the message of the Gospel. Colonization was assumed as the spiritual dispenser of light and liberty.

Edinburgh called for unity and concentration of missionary work. Its call for world evangelization was mainly directed to missionaries who came from the colonized continents of Africa and Asia. With the singleminded focus on evangelizing "the heathens" in colonized lands, the physical concerns of the colonized were brushed aside. When Bishop Azariah from India spoke about the unequal relationship that existed between missionaries and native Christians due to "the wrong structures of . . . western missions and the growing Asian churches," it was conveniently put aside.[287]

No individual or organizational effort was made to mend the existing inequality. Since the embittered relationship could not halt furtherance of the subsequent mission's cause, Bishop Azariah's plea was not heeded to in any of the mission conferences or in mission fields. The master-slave relationship that existed between missionaries and native Christian leaders has been narrated by Michael Hollis in his book *Paternalism and the Church.*[288]

The missionaries' close association with government officials, who helped the missions, heightened the significant presence of missionaries among converts and the missionaries' ultimate desire of making the converts loyal to the crown. The close association with government officials helped the missionaries observe "social

---

286. *The History and Records of the World Missionary Conference,* 1910, 9 vols. (Edinburgh: Oliphant, Anderson & Ferrier/New York: Revell, 1910), vol. 9, p. 145.

287. Hans-Ruedi Weber, *Asia and the Ecumenical Movement* (London: SCM Press Ltd., 1966), p. 118.

288. Michael Hollis, *Paternalism and the Church* (London: Oxford University Press, 1962).

distinction with considerable rigidity."[289] They were able to justify their racial superiority. The German missionaries, because of race and color, defended the caste system in India.

Eventually this feeling of superiority created duplicity in ministerial practice. For instance, the diary of Bishop Daniel Wilson of Calcutta shows that

> Having announced that there were to be no caste distinctions in the receiving of Holy Communion, he went on to say that the Europeans were to come first, then the respectable Indians from whatever community, and finally the servants.[290]

The existence of asymmetrical relationships between missionaries and converts in the mission field has been discussed in detail by Michael Hollis, not only in the area of worship and ecclesiastical prerogatives, but also in the area of finances and leadership.

The missionaries controlled the finances, and they set the salary scale for native Christian leaders, be it Bishop or catechist. The basic salary set by the missionaries for a native Bishop in India was three hundred rupees. (Note: William Carey was paid one thousand rupees for his part-time teaching position in Calcutta over one hundred years ago.) Some of the pastors had to live in the servants' quarters. The foreign-educated native leaders were refused the handshake of Europeans. Above all, when C.F.Andrews raised his voice to appoint an Indian as the Principal of St.Stephen's College, Delhi, it created a sensation among missionaries.[291]

Because of their close allegiance to the ruling race's ideologies and political thought, colonial missionaries forgot to render nationhood to native Christians and selfhood to converts. As for the mission conferences, Edinburgh and other IMC Conferences failed to give serious thought to the freedom struggle of the colonized masses and the request for nationalization of the church in India. Political liberation, human rights issues, and social development were given little importance. The conference leaders considered Christianity the fulfillment of all religions and continued to uphold the theory that non-Christian religions and Eastern

---

289. Ibid., p. 49.
290. Ibid., p. 50.
291. Ibid., pp. 48ff.

cultures were non-salvific and that Christianity alone, in Western form, would redeem them.

After Edinburgh, changes in international politics began to erode the superiority of European power in the East. Russia's defeat by Japan gave new confidence to the struggling Asiatic nations. After the Spanish-American war of 1898-99, the United States began to rise as a power on the world scene. The onset of World War I and the war between Christian nations in Europe made the colonized people wonder about the religion the Europeans advocated. In India a renewed kind of nationalism began to sweep across the nation after the arrival of foreign-educated young men. For instance, Gandhi's return from South Africa and his doctrine of Satyagragha (non-violence) gave a great impetus. The native-educated B. G. Tilak's fiery speech on Swaraj (self-government) began to capture the minds of young and old alike. The nationalistic movement was embraced by people of all religious persuasions. Indian Christian leaders began to think yet more seriously about the possibility of indigenizing both the theology and ecclesiology of Christian missionary work.

Missiologically, V.S.Azariah was ordained as the first national bishop of the Anglican Church in India with the support of a liberal-minded missionary, Bishop Henry Whitehead of Madras, in 1912. Seventeen Asians attended the Edinburgh Conference and were considered "delegates of British and American mission societies." On their way back from Edinburgh, V.S.Azariah and G.S.Eddy resolved to work toward the formation of a national church. They met at Bishop Whitehead's house in Madras in 1912, and then in 1919 at Tranquebar where the Anglican Church and the South India United Church declared their intention to merge and drafted the historic "Tranquebar Manifesto."

In India V.S. Azariah's ordination was not supported by all missionaries. Before he left for Calcutta to be ordained as a bishop, Azariah was confronted by a missionary who said, "I only hope you do as little harm to the Church of India as you can.[292] On the international scene, the Asian delegates were not allowed to represent their churches, but only admitted as delegates of British and American missions to the Edinburgh conference attended by over 1200 missionaries representing 159 societies.[293]

---

292. Carol Graham, *Azariah of Dornakal*, (London : SCM, 1946), p. 39.
293. Hans-Ruedi Weber, *Asia and Ecumenical Movement*, pp. 131, 137, 139.

After his episcopal ordination, Azariah became involved in the struggle for the indigenization of the church. G.S.Eddy, K.T.Paul, J.P.Jones, Bishop Whitehead, and a few others joined him in this venture. Their first phenomenal success was the union of the Anglican Church in India and the South India United Church represented by V.Santiago, M.Peter, and others, and the creation of "Indian Manifesto" in 1919. However, the leaders had to wait another 28 years before the historic Church of South India came into being in 1947.[294]

In the midst of a viable church union movement, the theological struggle for indigenization was causing confusion among Christians in India and other Asian countries. The problem of indigenization of Christian theology was discussed at the Jerusalem Conference in 1928. The years between the Jerusalem and Tambaram conferences were filled with debates concerning the salvific elements present in other religious faiths. William Hocking's liberal theological position in favor of non-Christian religions was violently opposed by Hendrick Kraemer, a conservative theologian serving as a missionary in Indonesia.

In a paper presented at the Jerusalem Conference, P. Chenchiah, a Hindu convert from Madras, narrated the challenges Hinduism was posing to Christianity.

> While Christianity is challenging Hinduism at the base, Hinduism is challenging Christianity at the top. When we ask Hinduism what it has done for the depressed and down-trodden classes, Hinduism meets us with the counter question. What have Christians to say to the first fruit of Hindu religion and culture? It is not enough to assert that Christ is unique. We should be able to say wherein He is unique that the world may see and appreciate it . . . The power of Christ which the Church manifests is a power which Hinduism feels is available within itself. Have we saints? So has Hinduism. Have we men at peace with God? So have they. Have we men who fight for righteousness? So have they also.[295]

---

294. Bengt Sundkler, *Church of South India*, pp. 41 ff.
295. *The Jerusalem Meeting of the I.M.E. March 24 - April 8, 1928*, 8 vols. (London: I.M.E., 1928) [referred to as the Jerusalem Report], vol. 1, pp. 360-1.

K.T.Paul was displeased with the comparison of values that Chenchiah was making. He contended that Christ was enough for India and that the message of Christ should be interpreted through human life and relationship. Organized Christianity alone was not enough to carry on the work of Christ. "Therefore it was necessary for missions to be fellow workers with Christ both inside and outside of organized Christianity."[296]

However, C.Y.Cheng of China summarized the debate of indigenization when he said,

The Christian Church does not exist for the sake of being indigenous. When you have solved the problem of making the Christian Church indigenous in China you have not solved the main problem of the Church.[297]

The Christians in India felt that they were left out of the freedom movement. They were becoming aware that the religion that they had come to love and to be part of was foreign in manifestation. Hence, they resolved to communicate the Christian message to the people of India by standing on a neutral ground and by utilizing common cultural terminologies. Hence they set indigenization of the Christian message at the top of their agenda. One of the first one to enter into the task of indigenizing the Christian theology was Bishop A.J.Appassamy of Coimbatore.

Meanwhile, anti-Western and anti-Christian feeling deepened in the 1920s after the Caliph of Islam was deposed in 1923 and after the British conquered Turkey. The Jallianwala massacre was traced back to Miss Sherwood, the missionary, who was jostled from her bicycle. Gandhi's non-violence movement and civil disobedience took a new turn when more and more educated young men began to join the liberation front. The Indian National Congress began to press for more power. The Round-Table Conferences were not taking the leaders anywhere. The worldwide depression, the failure of the League of Nations, the rise of Japanese power, and the religious renaissance began to cause irreparable damage to the political credibility and leadership capability of the Christian West.

296. Jerusalem Report, vol. 1, p. 362.
297. Jerusalem Report, vol. 3, p. 165.

Such changes in historical, political, and economic circumstances affected the growth of the church in India as well. Earlier, the socially oppressed people flocked into the church to express their dissatisfaction with their own traditional society, religion, culture, and ethnic background and in order to share the advantages Christianity was offering. As converts to Christianity they had access to Christian schools missionaries favor, Christian instruction and social liberation. The Christians were taught that in Christ all people are equal. The converts' social or economic or caste background would not matter in the sight of God. Now they had to bear the taunting stigma as "missionaries' running dogs," "rice Christians," and followers of a foreign religion. As a result, the Christians were left to themselves to work out their own future destiny.

When the Tambaram Conference was convened in 1938, it was preoccupied with Barthian theology, neo-orthodox ecclesiology and European political ideologies. The Conference was dominated by the conservative missionary theologians who asserted radical discontinuity of Christian religion from other religious faiths. The Indian Christian identity, the future of the church in India and the Indian people's struggle for political freedom were never taken seriously enough to be discussed. The Conference came to an abrupt end as World War II broke out. Both the missionaries and the colonizers, once again assumed the permanent presence of British government in India. They affirmed that the caste system, Hindu-Muslim religious feuds, 'the linguistic polyglot, cultural oppression of women, and so on, would partition the country and hence independence and self-rule should be denied. Since Europeans could not comprehend the moral force of the Gandhian non-violence movement, missionaries and administrators alike said that political independence on Gandhian lines would destroy the civilization and religion that they had introduced into India.

The missionaries continued to cling to the theology that they imported from Europe, and created an unappealing ecclesiastical deadlock and missiological standoff. When they found themselves being challenged in and outside the church, they resorted to maintaining the religious *status quo*. The people that they had to confront were not spiritually willing, physically submissive, or socially self-effacing any more. They asked for human dignity and political independence. The European mission theology became inadequate to meet the demand. As a result, Indian Christians had to live in a cultural and spiritual limbo for another decade until the Church of South India was formed.

Colonial Theology and Cultural Missiology

The European theology during the colonial period could not look beyond its geographical boundaries to take into account the struggles of the people for independence and freedom. By limiting the Gospel to one particular form of expression and ignoring contextualization of the good news, colonial missiology exiled the biblical concept of mission to an unknown future.

Theology is formed in historical, social, and cultural situations. It is a human reflection on divine events. It is human-made. Helmut Thielicke wrote, "Theology is a very human business, a craft, and sometimes an art." [298] It is expressed in human words for human purposes. Gordon D. Kauffman wrote,

> Theology is done by humans for human purposes; theological work must be assessed by human standards, and its judges are themselves always ordinary human beings.[299]

All of theology's assertions are limited; the work of the theologian is neither complete nor absolute. This was correctly defined by H. Richard Niebuhr when he wrote,

> Whatever be the case in other human inquiries there is no such thing as disinterestedness in theology, since no one can speak of God or gods at all save as valued beings or values which cannot be apprehended save by a willing, feeling, responding self.[300]

Because of the presence of human elements, every theology is limited and finite. No one can produce an objective and absolute theology. And hence, Niebuhr continued,

---

298. Helmut Thielicke, *A Little Exercise for Young Theologians*, trans. Charles L. Taylor (Grand Rapids, Mich: Eerdmans, 1962), p. 37.
299. Gordon D. Kauffman, "Theological Method and Indigenization: Six Theses," *Shepher'd Staff*, No. 44 (June 1977), p. 6.
300. H. Richard Niebuhr, *The Meaning of Revelation* (New York: Macmillan Co., 1947), p. 35.

Though we direct our thought to eternal and transcendent beings, it is not eternal and transcendent, though we regard the universal, the image of the universal in our mind is not a universal image.[301]

Due to its limitation to a specific context and time, theology is to be deemed only a reflection of a particular people's own cultural, social, and spiritual expression of God and the universe, be it European or Asian. Paul Tillich wrote, "Every religious act, not only in organized religions, but also in the most intimate movement of the soul, is culturally formed."[302] Since theological expressions are culturally formed, Tillich says, religion and its symbols "have their roots in the totality of human experience including local surroundings, in all their ramifications, both political and economic."[303]

The colonial theology was conditioned by European political thought and shaped by its cultural elements. The intellectual path that the mission historians and the missionaries often followed in India was drawn from the scientific and colonial theories that were predominant in Europe at the close of the nineteenth century. In fact the missionaries upheld many of the Orientalists' epithets about India in their missiological narratives. The letters, the journals, and the reports that they produced reflect the colonial structure in which they were delivered. The missionaries profess themselves to be authentic, unerring, and well influenced, yet all-encompassing. Analyzed deeply, the narrative structure proves itself to be one-sided and geographically limited. It was built upon specific situations where certain details were amplified and others carefully omitted. The sheer organic strength of the colonial mission's discourse, and its very close ties to the socio-economic colonial political institutions, has been a considerable material investment.

This idea of religious expressions and its socio-economic political ramification was summarized by Ludwig Feuerbach in his book *The Essence of Christianity* when he said that theology was human

---

301. Ibid., 10.
302. Paul Tillich, *Theology and Culture*, ed. Robert C. Kimball (New York: Oxford University Press, 1959), p. 42.
303. Paul Tillich, *The Future of Religions,* ed. Jerald C. Brauer, (New York: Harper & Row, 1966), p. 93.

reflection of an eternal being in a definite place, history, and culture. To him, "theology is anthropology."[304]

Being produced in a human cultural context with the help of divine revelation, theology is concerned with good and evil, light and darkness, God and Satan, divine and human. In the colonial context, it was concerned with conversion and evangelism. Paul Tillich wrote,

> The "situation" theology must consider is the creative interpretation of existence, an interpretation which is carried on in every period of history under all kinds of psychological and sociological emotions ... The "situation" to which theology must respond is the totality of man's creative self-interpretation in a special period.[305]

Unfortunately, the colonial mission chose to ignore the converts' total need and overlooked their struggle for independence and liberation from political and economic oppression. Having taken the side of the colonizers openly, colonial missiology became a parochial, convenient, and political missiology. Since the human situational context determines the formation of theology and serves the needs of the Christian community, the Christian messenger must respond to the total needs of the listening community.[306]

Karl Barth summarized it precisely when he wrote, "Dogmatics is a theological discipline. But theology is a function of the church."[307] In short, theological teaching must be comprehensive, responsible and redemptive. As the church provides the context for doing theology, the theologian has to be in touch with the people of the church community where the action takes place and with a source of revelation that provides healing to the broken and battered community. The dual contact the theologian maintains within the redeemed community helps him to connect the temporal and the eternal, and to interpret the message from above within

---

304. Ludwig Feuerbach, *The Essence of Christianity,* trans. George Eliot (New York: Harper Torchbooks, 1957), pp. vii-xxx.

305. Paul Tillich, *Systematic Theology,* vol. 1(Chicago: University of Chicago Press, 1951), p. 4.

306. Ibid., p. 3.

307. Karl Barth, *Church Dogmatics,* i trans. G.T. Thompson (Edinburgh: T & T Clark, 1936), p. 1.

the people's context. This hermeneutical task of the theologian was summarized by Tillich.

> A theological system is supposed to satisfy two needs: the statement of the truth of the Christian message and interpretation of this truth for every generation. Theology moves back and forth between two poles, the eternal truth of its foundation and the temporal situation in which the eternal truth must be received.[308]

In short, in his hermeneutical consciousness of the interpretation of the Gospel, the messenger is seeking to adhere to the delicate balance of the social existence of human living, divine revelation, and biblical narrative. The human living situation has to be understood thoroughly in order to interpret the revealed message properly. Culture, habits, language and traditions must be taken seriously in order to understand human living conditions. Outside elements cannot be superimposed on them. Theology must evolve out of interaction between those human elements and divine experience that occurs in each cultural context.

In colonial missiology God was limited to the theological origin of its advocates and the missiological benefits of its sponsors. Hence an adequate distinction between divine revelation and human aspirations had to be made clear in order to understand the methodology of colonial missiology. The colonial mission was molded by the European Christian tradition and hence it attempted to transplant one particular form of spiritual expression to people of another culture.[309]

In effect the colonial missionaries' interpretation of the Gospel, their formation of theological statements and their execution of missiological ideas were limited by the missionaries' socio-cultural standpoint and their personal experience. This idea was well illustrated by James D. Smart.

> (The interpretation) begins before we are conscious of doing anything other than words. We hear them in a context, a

---

308. Tillich, *Systematic Theology*, vol. 1, p. 3.
309. See H. Richard Niebuhr, *Christ and Culture* (New York: Harper Torch Books, 1956), p. 2.

highly complex context, the total context of our present historical existence. We hear them as the persons that we are, and their meaning for us is determined not only by the words but the character of the context in which we receive them. No man has direct access to the content of Scripture either by the perfection of his scholarship or the power of his inspiration. Every apprehension of the text and every statement of its meaning is an interpretation and, however adequately it expresses the content of the text, it dare not ever be equated with the text itself.[310]

The missionaries were concerned with ensuring that Indian Christians received the correct pattern of behavior, right set of doctrines, and the true model of church order which were developed in Europe. In their enthusiasm for the permanence of the church in India, they attempted to transplant the European church to India, not knowing that India, unlike other colonized lands, had its own advanced language systems, philosophical thought, critical theories, and religious literatures rich and advanced vocabularies for the understanding and expression of abstract, philosophical, and religious thought. They resorted to the easy way of imposing European language, culture, and religious thought on India, as their thinking was conditioned by their political environment.

This idea of culture conditioning of the message was attested to by Abraham Heschel and Kosuke Koyama when they said that the meaning and value of cultures are important for the development of history and theology. Heschel wrote,

What concerns the prophet is the human event as a divine experience. History to us is the record of human experience; to the prophet it is a record of God's experience.[311]

Kosuke Koyama added,

Human history is always cultural. A denuded a-cultural history is an impossibility. That history is a record of God's experience

---

310. James D. Smart, *The Strange Silence of the Bible in the Church: A Study in Hermeneutics* (London: S.C.M. Press, 1970), pp. 53-54.
311. Abraham J. Heschel, *The Prophets* (New York: Harper & Row, 1962), p. 172.

implies an interrelatedness that is present between theology and culture.[312]

As I have mentioned earlier, the message of the colonial mission was the product of the missionaries living in the dominant colonial context. Their thinking was shaped, their theology expressed, and their missiology conceptualized within the colonial structure. By equating Western culture with Christ and Christianity, the colonial missiology defined the essence of Christianity in one particular form of expression, and ignored explaining it in terms of the natives' pain and suffering. The mission organizations were so bound to the social *a priori* of colonial structure that the liberation of the colonized was at best a peripheral theme. It was within this context that the relationship between the natives and the Europeans was sustained; the activities of the community were influenced; human dignity was realized. The European missionaries could not exempt themselves from responsibility for the social and political implications of their work. There was no neutral, value-free zone from which they could carry out their missionary goal.

The asymmetrical relationship that existed between the missionaries and the converts gave rise to native converts who existed as marginal human beings on the field, being deprived of their Christian national identity as well as viable means of achieving political freedom and national independence. In essence the colonial mission accommodated itself to the views of the *conquistadors*[313] in the twentieth century and made a serious attempt to plant the European church in India without caring for the physical needs of the people. As a result, colonial missiology became a "designer missiology" (European, colonial, political, and existential form) and took the form of European evangelical ethnocentrism.

Furthermore, the European evangelical ideology gave rise to the idea of total abhorrence of non-European cultures, religions, and traditions. The absolute rejection of another culture's language, religion, habits, and spirituality led the missionaries to believe in the universality of their ethnocentric particularism and to overlook

---

312. Kosuke Koyama, *Mount Fuji and Mount Sinai* (New York; Orbis Books, 1984), p. 5.
313. Cf. G. Voss, Missionary Accommodation," in *Missionary Academic Study*, No. 2 (New York: Faith, 1946), p. 17.

the need to contextualize the Gospel.[314] Because of the inadequate development of the theology of colonial mission and its improper use in evangelizing the natives, the missionaries identified God with a particular form of historical, political movement and rejected local cultures and freedom movements. The sanction of Christian theology was conveniently identified with the idea of "the white man's burden" and the "imperial" civilizing mission.[315]

In "Theology of Imperialism" Max Warren delineates God's active involvement in secular history.[316] M.M.Thomas vehemently opposes this and cites how the Confessing Church in Nazi Germany condemned the identification of God with the particular movement of secular history.[317] That opposition was echoed in the New Delhi Conference. It affirmed that

> No earthly kingdom can set itself . . . up as the Kingdom of God on earth, and no political ambition is wholly conformed to the divine purpose.[318]

Missionaries during the nineteenth century interpreted the gospel according to their cultural and political interest. By identifying themselves with the dominant exterior power structure and submitting themselves to European cultural projections, they limited the dynamics of the Gospel. The colonizers' political oppression of the colonized was not given an important part in the missionaries' theological agenda; the hegemonic imposition of European culture, language and civilization upon the India people was not considered a missiological issue. Conversion of individual souls alone occupied the missionaries. Pope Paul VI said,

---

314. See Paul A. Cohen, *China and Christianity: The Missionary Movement and the Growth of Chinese Antiforeignism 1860-1870* (Cambridge: Harvard University Press, 1974). Although the word contextualization was a relatively new word in twentieth century mission circles, the practice of the term was not new to the missionaries. The method was adopted in its fullest sense in mission fields by missionaries such as Matteo Ricci, Adam Schall, Ferdinand Verbiest, Robert de Nobili and others.
315. See Klaus E. Knorr, *British Colonial Theories*, pp. 266-7, 366, 376-88, 404.
316. Max Warren, *Caesar: The Beloved Enemy* (London: S.C.M.Press, 1955).
317. M.M.Thomas, *The Christian Response to the Asian Revolution* (London: S.C.M.Press, 1966), pp. 9-34.
318. *The New Delhi Report,* The Third Assembly of the W.C.C. 1961 (London: S.C.M Press, 1962), p. 85.

The Church evangelizes when she seeks to convert, solely through the divine power of the Message she proclaims, both the personal and collective consciences of people, the activities in which they engage, and the lives and concrete milieus which are theirs.[319]

Conversion cannot be brought about through authoritarian dictation, nor can it be realized through various forms of European cultural romanticism; it can be achieved only by reconciling human beings with human beings, and human beings with God. In that process it respects human identity and recognizes human dignity. Human aspirations and fuller expression of human potentialities are valued and recognized. The Gospel convicts and liberates human beings from sin and oppressive forces. The Good News has been revealed from above, but speaks to the context. The message of the New Testament reassures the suffering Children of God with eschatological hope which originates from here and now.

Since mission theology comes out of the interaction of human elements with divine events at the local cultural matrix, and it evolves out of the daily struggles of human beings, true identification with their social living, active participation in their struggle for freedom, and total involvement in their efforts toward eschatological liberation become prerequisites for the formation of a theology of mission. Failing to do so will result in a reinterpretation and reconsideration of the superimposed and supercultural theology.[320] Authentic Christian mission tries to encourage the cultural history of the people and attempts to promote the biblical reality of human redemption.

Since nineteenth-century colonial missiology was a "cultural missiology," its manifested form was not in any way considered superior to Christianity as observed by the Malabar Christians in South India, or to the national church which Narayan Tilak, Bishop Azariah, and other national Christian leaders were practicing and trying to advocate.

319. *Evangelii Nuntiandi* (On Evangelism in the Modern World) 8 December 1975, para 28.
320. See Eugene A. Nida, *Message and Mission: The Communication of Christian Faith* (New York: Harper, 1960), pp. 171ff. Also Charles Kraft, "Ideological Factors in Intercultural Communication," *Missiology An International Review*, 2 (July 1974), pp. 295-312.

Colonial mission dealt with only a part of the biblical reality of mission. Conversion of individual souls was considered the end of mission; rather, it is the initial task for the ultimate goal of liberating people from the bondage of sin, exploitation, and oppression. The biblical message of mission is that all human beings are created in the image of God, redeemed by Christ, and called of God to a task beyond history in order to sustain and interpret the very purpose of human existence. In the process the church enriches the communities while the church itself is being enriched; and the church instills the eschatological hope of ultimate redemption from darkness, bondage and sin.

The eschatological message of redemption and freedom is not to be understood as a future event or an otherworldly affair, but rather as the divine intervention that breaks into the present social context of the struggling masses longing to be free. The message of liberation and the activities of mission make the people aware that the colonizers' mode of oppression contradicts the will of God as defined by the eschatological nature of God. Therefore, the eschatological hope should not diminish, but should stimulate the importance of Christians' active involvement in the affairs of the present world where God's plans are being fulfilled by human beings who are made in the image of God.

Contextual theology does not reject everything that is Western. After all indigenized Eastern Christian principles have their Western origin. Contextual theology goes beyond indigenization. Indigenization is the precursor of contextualizing Western theology into a non-Western context. Contextual theology is the outcome of Christian faith's interaction with the local culture's spiritual elements and the expression of the Christian message of hope in the listeners' context of pain and struggle. Contextualization takes the biblical message of the God of all Nations seriously. God is not the respecter of persons. In Isaiah 19:24-25 God speaks of "Egypt my people, and Assyria the work of my hands, and Israel my heritage."

Contextualizing Christian message is to present the paschal mystery of Christ as the determining factor in the complexity of human life. The message of the cross as redemptive and exemplary challenges human values and cultural patterns. Its visible expression is not death, but resurrection; its manifested form is not bondage, but liberation. Having faith in the redemptive

significance of Christ's vicarious death on the cross has the
constitutive elements of liberation and justice. Faith in the paschal
mystery of Christ is a forward movement and an eschatological hope. The culmination of this movement is the kingdom
of God.

As much as the followers of Christ are called to participate in
the death and sufferings of Christ, they are invited to make their
faith present and actively involved in their relations with people
in history. Christian involvement in the struggle for justice is an
expression of the presence of God's grace and the affirmation of
the eschatological hope of Christians.

The demands of justice and liberation are generally interpreted
in particular ways because of a culturally, historically, socially
conditioned model. Class, gender and race play vital roles in the
demands and execution of justice. The message of Jesus Christ
was a call for justice and liberation, a demand for concern for the
poor and the deliverance of the oppressed. His commitment to
the message of the Gospel was a commitment to the praxis for
change. And for this very purpose, the church has reasons enough
to challenge the world and transcend cultural moorings.

However, justice cannot be achieved when the citizens are
prevented from sharing the decision-making power that decisively
shapes structures determining their economic, social, political
and spiritual reality. Precisely at this point both the missionaries
and the colonizers hesitated to consider the necessity of accepting
native leadership and political independence. Like their predecessors, the new generation of missionaries who came to India
in the twentieth century were not regarded as "spiritual parents"
by the native Christians. The converts did not like being treated
as spiritual infants, as during the days of the pioneer missionaries.
The Indian Christian leaders wanted a change in the theological,
ecclesiastical, and missiological policies of the missionary structure.
The missionaries' uncritical maintenance of the past caused tension
on the mission field. The missionaries seriously ignored the
eschatological hope of the kingdom of God seriously and continued
to promote what Johannes B. Metz calls "a softened eschatology."[321]

321. Johanness B. Metz, "For a Renewed Church before a New Council: A
Concept in Four Theses," in David Tracy (ed), *Toward Vatican III*, (New York:
The Free Press, 1978), p. 143.

CHAPTER X

Indian Politics and Missionary Response

The Home Rule Movement in India existed even before Gandhi entered into the political arena, although it confined itself mainly to large towns and cities. As the majority of the rural population was unaffected by the movement, both the missionaries and government assumed that British rule in India was not disliked by all the people.[322] The Missionary Review of the world reported in April 1918,

> It must not be forgotten, as we study the movement of the hour, that the great mass of Indian people are very slightly, if at all touched by them. They are appalled at the suggestion of the extremists that he and his fellows should supplant the man from the west. It is therefore fair to say that the general currents of the life of the country are as yet little changed.[323]

Missionary accounts of life in India were full of contemptuous expressions about the then prevailing caste system. Caste system in India was so intriguing to Westerners that they built their political and missiological *episteme* on it. Even political freedom was denied because of the social role caste played in Indian society. *The Missionary Review of the World* asserted, "Home Rule can not be successful where caste prevails."[324] Supporting the British, Father Brenton T. Bradley wrote in 1920 that the caste system and democracy cannot coexist in India.[325]

> The three greatest factors contributing to India's progress are the Bible, the English language and modern education. England has been back of all three, and these have struck at what has always been typical of the old, undemocratic India. England

---

322. *The Literary Digest* 65 (May 1920): p. 58.
323. *The Missionary Review of the World* 41 (April 1918): p. 242.
324. Ibid., p. 243.
325. *The World Outlook* 6 (July 1920): p. 11.

has built democracy into India's thinking. Let us not slash her in order to get a striking setting for India's claims.[326]

The statement betrays not only the nescience of Fr. Bradley but also a biased misunderstanding of a colonized people. Any serious student of Indian affairs would know that British colonial rule in India was anything but democratic. The newly arrived American missionaries and the already present British missionaries predicted that if Britain abandoned India, Brahmin oligarchy, Mohammedan invaders, and Maratha warriors would demolish what British trusteeship had established since Plassey in 1757.[327]

However, after the end of World War I, the political situation in India took a different turn. The introduction of Rowlatt Bills, which ultimately became an act of the Central Government, created much disturbance among the people of India. The first part of the Rowlatt Bills was an amendment of the Indian Penal Code of Criminal Procedure of 1898; the second part made provision for emergency powers for the Government, supplementing the Ordinary Criminal Law in special circumstances. Under the provisions of the Bills, anyone in possession of any document— with the intention of circulation or publication— containing word, sign, or visible representation which could instigate, whether directly or indirectly, the use of criminal force against the Government or any public servant would be punished with imprisonment.[328] The bills gave enormous power to the British authorities to stop, question, and arrest any citizen of India.

The provisions of the Bills were opposed by Mahatma Gandhi who testified before the Hunter Commission, which was instituted to inquire into the Amritsar Massacre. He said,

When the Rowlatt bills were published I felt that they were so restrictive of human liberty that they must be restricted to the utmost. I observed, too, that the opposition to them was universal among Indians. I submit that no state, however

---

326. Ibid.

327. Price Collier, *The West in the East* (New York: Charles Scriner's Sons, 1911), p. 97.

328. Pattabhi Sittaramayya, *History of the Indian National Congress*, vol. 1 (Bombay: Patma Publications, 1966), p. 157.

despotic, has the right to enact laws which are repugnant to the whole body of the people, much less a government guided by constitutional usages and precedent such as the Indian government.[329]

The Rowlatt Act, which was a humiliating blow to the Indians, did not get the support of the missionaries and their societies. They assumed that the act was simply intended to strengthen the hands of the administrators, and to subdue the undesirable activities of misguided people, and that loyal citizens need have no fear. There is hardly any reference to missionary opposition to human rights violations or critical remarks concerning the oppression of an alien power by legal and political means.

On hearing the introduction of the Rowlatt Bills in the Central Legislature in 1919, Gandhi published a pledge to begin his Passive Resistance or *Satyagraha*.

Being conscientiously of the opinion that the Bills known as the Indian Criminal Law Amendment Bill No.1 of 1919 and the Criminal Law Emergency Powers Bill No.2 of 1919 are unjust, subversive of the principles of liberty and justice, and destructive of the elementary rights of an individual on which the safety of India as a whole and the state itself is based, we solemnly affirm that in the event of these Bills becoming law and until they are withdrawn, we refuse civilly to obey these laws and such other laws as the committee to be hereafter appointed may think fit, and we further affirm that in the struggle we will faithfully follow truth and refrain from violence to life, person or property. [330]

Before Gandhi could launch his *Satyagraha*, events took a serious turn in the Punjab when two popular leaders, Saif-ud-Din Kichlew, an advocate, and Satyapal, a medical practitioner, were deported. When the public went to the house of the Deputy Commissioner with a petition to ask for the release of their two

329. Mohanlal Karamchand Gandhi, *Young India — 1919-22* (New York: B.W. Huelisch Inc., 1923), p. 11.
330. *India in 1919*, a statement prepared for presentation to Parliament under the requirement of the Government of India Act (Calcutta: Government of India Central Publication Branch, 1920), p. 27.

leaders, they were fired upon by the troops. Soon mob violence flared up, ending in the murder of some Englishmen. A missionary woman was jostled from her bicycle and sustained some injuries. The civil officials turned the town over to the army who imposed martial law. The situation began to get worse at Amritsar.

On April 13, 1919, the Hindu New Year Day, a large public meeting was held at a place called Jallianwala Bagh (an open ground in the center of the city), enclosed on all sides by the walls of houses and with only one narrow entrance. When about 20,000 men, women, and children had gathered there for a meeting, Brigadier-General R.E.H.Dyer entered the place and, in his own words, "to make a wide impression on the element of discontent in the Punjab," ordered his troops to fire on the unarmed crowd. According to the official report, over 400 were killed and about 1500 wounded in ten minutes. The wounded were left overnight to die without care or attendance, resulting in more deaths the following day.

When the Hunter Committee was appointed to investigate the massacre, General Dyer replied, "I could have dispersed the crowd without firing, but they would have come back again and laughed, and I should have made what I considered to be a fool of myself."[331] The military rule in the Punjab caused more misery after the incident. Water and electricity were cut off in Amritsar. Public flogging became common. All Indians passing along the street where the missionary woman had been knocked down from her bicycle were made to crawl on their bellies. When General Dyer was asked about his crawling order, he replied,

> We look upon women as sacred. I searched in my mind for a form of punishment that would meet this action. I did not know how to meet it. I felt the street should be looked upon as sacred, . . . no Indians shall pass along here and there and if they have to pass they must do so on all fours. It never entered my mind that any man in his senses would voluntarily go through that street.[332]

The Hunter Commission appointed by the Viceroy to investigate

---

331. P. Sittaramayya, *History of the Indian National Congress*, p. 105.
332. *The Literary Digest* 64 (June 24, 1920): p. 25.

the massacre proved to be inadequate and partial. While newspapers in the East and the West were critical of the Commission's reports and findings, the missionary journals reported that the rebels were mainly the discontented Muslims, Hindus and Sikhs. One particular press was critical of the Commission and the British administration itself. The editor of the paper was critical of the accepted tactics that British troops had developed in maintaining permanent British rule by force, even if every Indian died in the process.

Of course, says the report in effect, bombing villages from airplanes sometimes results in the death of innocent persons, and this is deplorable; but in general, it is a method we feel called upon to approve. Of course, if people assembled in an illegal gathering refuse to disperse they must be fired upon, but it is worthwhile even at the expense of several seconds' time to order them to disperse before killing them. Thus have argued tyrants and their apologists in all ages. When the Czar shot down hundreds of peaceful petitioners "illegally assembled" before the Winter Palace in January 1905, he doubtless argued as the Hunter Commission argues with regard to Amritsar. When the Germans dropped bombs on British babies in English villages they doubtless urged same necessity that forces English airmen to drop bombs on Indian babies in defenseless villages in the Punjab. The history of atrocity and the history of autocratic military rule are one and the same. And the nation which builds that sort of history, be it Russian or German or British or American, is doomed to the horror of war with its neighbours and to rebellion at home.[333]

Unfortunately, the mission societies never raised their voice against the massacres in Amritsar, Lahore, and Jallianwallabagh. As a result, then and now, Punjab and several northern provinces in India have become unresponsive to the preaching of the Gospel. The people in those provinces continue to associate Christianity with the British or alien colonial power.

The negative consequences of the Rowlatt Act, the massacre at Jallianwallabagh and the launching of *Satyagraha* emotionally

---

333. *The Nation* 110 (June 19, 1920): p. 814.

integrated the Hindu and Muslim communities in India to resist
alien rule. As a result, Gandhi emerged as one, a single strong
and national leader, both for the Hindus and Muslims. He started
the non-cooperation movement and gave the people the slogan,
"*Swaraj* within a year".[334] Commenting on the stormy days in
India, Majumdar wrote,

> Amritsar, Lahore, Jallianwalla massacres, indiscriminate
> arrests, trials and convictions which recall the days of Jeffreys
> in England followed . . . India lost faith in England.[335]

During this time the Christians in India tried to disassociate
themselves from the Western missionaries and tried to indigenize
their faith. A few native Christian leaders got involved in politics.
Babu Kali Charan Banaerji took an active part in the Congress.
Reverend D.L.Joshi, a national Christian leader from Bombay,
cried, "Awake, Indian Christians. *Swadeshism* is in the air. Is it
without lesson for us?"[336] Christians across the nation supported
the Gandhian movement.

Indian Christian theologians felt that the Church in India
should be missionary-minded and the Christian community should
develop eclectic theology without Western confessional teaching.
A.J.Appasamy demonstrated a fresh approach to Indian Christian
theology by citing mystic elements in Johannine Gospel and
comparing them with the Bhakti marga (devotional path) in
Hinduism. Later, he was joined by P.Chenchiah and his brother-
in-law V. Chakkarai Chetty, lawyers and lay theologians from
Madras. They formed a Christian Book Club and the Christo
Samaj, a counter-organization to Brahmo Samaj. Their fundamental argument was that if Christianity as practiced by the
Europeans has incorporated Hebrew tradition, Greek philosophy,
and continental existentialism, Eastern Christianity could also
borrow from its local, cultural, and philosophical traditions to
enrich Christianity and make it relevant to the Christian's cultural

---

334. A.K.Majumdar, *Advent of Independence*, (Bombay: Bharatya Vidya Bhavan,
1963), pp. 88-89.
335. R.C.Majumdar, *The History and Culture of the Indian People's Struggle for
Freedom* (Bombay: Raman, 1969), p. 443.
336. "A Call to Indian Christians," *Church Missionary Intelligencer*, March
1906, p. 195.

milieu.[337] They all argued that the local cultural, and native philosophical ideas as well as native religious sentiments should be taken seriously into account in interpreting the Biblical concept of salvation. By doing so, they argued, the outward form of the message may vary from culture to culture, while the core biblical message would remain intact and understood in a non-Western way.[338]

The imported and modified Student Volunteer Movement's slogan, "Evangelization of India in this generation," was pushed aside. K.T. Paul, V.S. Azariah, and V.Santiago planned together to indigenize all the mission and outreach organizations; and eventually the National Missionary Society was formed.[339] After returning from Edinburgh, V.S. Azariah was consecrated as an Anglican bishop and sent to Dornakal as a missionary bishop.

In May 1919 the India Ministers' Conference was held in Tranquebar. With two Western missionaries present, Azariah chaired the meeting (for the first time in history) and discussed the indigenization of the church in India. After much discussion and deliberation, the leaders of the church, particularly V. Santiago and M. Peter of the South India United Church and V.S. Azariah of the Anglican Church, accepted a resolution on the union of the two major denominations, which came to be known as the "Tranquebar Manifesto", and which paved the way for the formation of the Church of South India in 1947.

The united Church was formed in order to move along with the demands of Indian political movement and to sever all non-

---

337. Oscar Cullman, for instance, says Western Christian theology borrowed concepts such as spirit, matter; and immortality of the soul from Greek philosophy. See Oscar Cullman, *Immortality of the Soul or Resurrection of the Dead? The Witness of the New Testament* (London: Epworth Press, 1959).

338. The very thought of taking local culture seriously was understood by P. Devanandam, M.M. Thomas, T.V. Philip and others after the independence of India in 1947. The Christianity and civilization, they argued, that the European missionaries attempted to thrust upon the Indian people was an individualistic type and imperialistic in nature. It has to be replaced with the passive, Indian cultural, political, historical and metaphysical descriptions of thought and understanding of the Gospel. See T.V.Philip, "Christianity in India During Western Colonialism: Conflict, Reconciliation, or Adjustment," *The Indian Church History Review*, 1987, pp. 16ff.

339. Bengt Sundkler, *Church of South India*, p. 34.

essential ties with the European West which imposed divisions
among the people of India. The Manifesto declares,

> We believe that the challenge of the present hour in the
> period of reconstruction after the war in the gathering together
> of the nations, and the present critical situation in India itself,
> call us to mourn our past divisions and turn to our Lord
> Jesus Christ to seek in Him the unity of the body expressed
> in one visible Church. We face together the titanic task of the
> winning of India for Christ— one fifth of the human race. Yet,
> confronted by such an overwhelming responsibility, we find
> ourselves rendered weak and relatively impotent by our
> unhappy divisions— divisions for which we were not responsible,
> and which have been, as it were, imposed upon us from without;
> divisions which we did not create, and which we do not
> perpetuate.[340]

The Tranquebar resolutions became the cornerstone for building
up the Church of South India. The indigenization of the Church
in India was carried out without the help of the European
missionaries. When critical issues had to be discussed and crucial
decisions had to be made, V.S.Azariah played a diplomatic role.
He eventually emerged out as the main architect of the citadel of
the Church of South India.[341] Ever since Gandhi emerged as a
national leader, the political situation in India has taken a different
turn. People from all religious, regional and ethnic backgrounds
joined together to fight for freedom and independence. Individual
European and American missionaries such as C.F.Andrews and
E.Stanley Jones became close friends of Gandhi and began to
support the Indian national movements. The mission societies
began to concentrate their work among "receptive" communities
and to consolidate their work for the day when they would have
to leave the fruits of their labor to the national Christian leaders
who would carry on the ministry.

Indian Christian identity, Indian nationalism, and demand
for political independence were made possible mainly because of
the political subjection of the Indian people by the British. Britain,

---

340. Ibid., p. 101.
341. Hans-Ruedi Weber, *Asia and the Ecumenical Movement*, p. 148.

for its own advantage, radically changed the cultural, religious, and political structure of Indian society, established a centralized state, promoted Christian religion, and introduced education and modern means of communication and transportation. This resulted in the emergence of new social and political classes, the unleashing of new cultural and religious forces, and the union of strange bedfellows. The association of the Hindu and Muslim communities during the independence struggle was unique in itself. The inauguration of the Church of South India was unprecedented in Christian history.

Conclusion

Several paradoxes regarding European colonization of India exist in written texts. One of these concerns the methods and ease of conquest of India. On the one hand, European historians noted that the conquest was peacefully accomplished, and that the Europeans were welcomed as a lesser evil than the Muslims who forcefully converted the Hindus, who looted their temple treasuries, and who violently ruled over them. Hence the Englishmen were looked upon as allies in times of feuds between native kings and seen as "liberators" from the Moghul rule. On the other hand, the people in India never thought that the European powers, with their "divide and rule" policy, would pit one king against the other and eventually become the sole rulers of the country for two hundred years.

When the native kings, both the Nizam (Muslim) and the Hindu rulers, rose against the East India Company, it became evident by the end of the eighteenth century that they were violently subdued and their territories unjustly annexed to the already conquered land by the colonial powers. In place of the former rulers, "puppet" kings were installed.

European historians, who relied mostly on the East Indian Company's report presented to the Board of Directors affirmed the popular European notions. One such notion was that the armed resistance in India in 1857 broke out mainly in Muslim territories and in regions with a long history of external aggression and raiding. The Mutiny of 1857 was not totally associated with the freedom movement or liberation struggle.

In every documented case the native resistance has been presented as a futile attempt by disgruntled Muslims and Hindus. A massive and united struggle against the British could not be mounted because of the extreme political fragmentation of Indian society which allowed the British to progressively meet and defeat the rebellious subjects. Cultural and linguistic division in India was attributed by the Europeans to political rivalries, Hindu or Muslim oligarchy, Indian illiteracy and backwardness in organizing a structured society.

The sole reason that the rest of the nation could not join the resistance groups in North India was the lack of communication and unavailability of transportation to mobilize native forces.

Distance played a major role in preventing the forces from the South from joining the mutineers. Furthermore, the frightful terror the Company soldiers with powerful guns and military power had planted among the native rulers and the general public had already spread fear and trepidation. The minor insurrections were quelled with excessive force and were forcefully contained to regions. The major "rebellion" in 1857, however, changed the course of the colonizers' history and hence several hypothesis were offered to the general public in Britain.

The colonial history under the Crown also was inharmonious and inconsistent. Although no open violence or rebellion had occurred during that period, the country was brooding for a storm. During the second half of the nineteenth century, the Hindu religious renaissance, the active role of Brahmo Samaj, Arya Samaj, the autonomous functions of Hindu colleges and institutions, the founding of the Indian National Congress, and the Hindu coalition with the Muslim party set the stage for Gandhi's arrival and his campaign of non-violence.

Northern India was more active than the southern region. The political resistance in the north was accompanied by an equal reluctance toward religious conversion which lasted until 1947. Missionaries were unsuccessful in religious conversion even though they settled among the people for long periods. In South India and other parts of the country, where there was no open resistance against the British, the mission societies enjoyed mass conversions. In all these instances religious belief and practice resulted from changes in the political structure which effectively enabled the mission to thrive or shrivel.

Although there is something basically appealing about the sacrifices and the painful efforts which the missionaries took in bringing the Gospel, in providing education and knowledge to people in India, and in their unquestionable integrity and intentionality in establishing the church in India, the appeal literally pales when their association with colonial structure is realized, and the mission's continued interplay with the European socio-political model is recognized. In carrying out the task of mission in the midst of one of the few culturally ancient, religiously polycrat, and philosophically opulent societies in the world, the missionaries were severely limited and confined by their chosen base of colonizing culture.

They simplified the problems that arose on the field. Every non-normative social entity (caste, brahminical order of societal structure, tribal and rural ceremonies and festivals, and so on) and non-European religious-cultural practice (idol worship, temple sacrifices, and so on) were exiled to an irreconcilable other. By refusing to acknowledge the profound cultural and religious value-practices of the heterogeneous entity called India, oft-times the mission societies failed to see the country's past, painful historical realities, the ambiguous richness of religious pluralism, communal loyalty and the magnificent hierarchy of "guru-shisya" (teacher-disciple) possibility. The refusal to accept native culture deprived the Gospel of being preached in its contextualizing nature and of its dynamics of penetrating every human society.

The missionaries who preached against caste were flawed when they themselves fell victims to the romantic notion of European racial superiority in a society that could not heal itself from the brahminical invention of caste. When seen in a deeper perspective, caste is a subtle form of racism. When this feeling of belonging to a higher kind was carried over to the twentieth century by the Europeans, the Indian people's political struggle and economic liberation were given secondary place. The people began to feel colonized forever. The Christians observed that they were doubly colonized: by the government and by the church structures.

In early the twentieth century missionaries talked about the necessity of indigenizing the church in India; but soon they lost sight of it as indigenization would demand sharing power, authority, leadership, and traditions.

An authentic cross-cultural mission is historical, cultural, eschatological, multi-vocal, and multi-racial. In other words, it is more than indigenization. It is contextual. In that sense the European mission became single-sided, one-shaded, and mono-dimensional. It continued certain normative structures brought from outside the soil of genuine mission activity.

Missionaries in the nineteenth century followed Western cultural norms and in practice they adapted well-tested European conventions. For instance, the cry for a black missionary by the people in Asia was never answered.[342] Had the mission societies,

---

342. Eric S. Fife and Arthur F. Glasser, *Mission in Crisis* (Wheaton, Ill: Inter Varsity Press, 1961), 155-6.

in their effort to indigenize the church, sent a few black missionaries to preach and evangelize, the history of mission in Asia and around the world would have been much different. What the colonized world had wanted during the time of oppression was the message of the crucified Lord and the encouragement of a fellow suffering church being narrated by a suffering people. A suppressed and a marginalized group, such as the black Christians in Europe or North America, could have given both the message and encouragement.

Two reasons have been given for not sending black missionaries to Asia: the existing government would deny them visas, and the black missionaries would be unable to adjust to the white missionaries.[343] Asia has always been open to diversity. Denial of visas for the entry of a people on the basis of their differentness traces back to the political powers, since most countries in Asia had already been colonized by European nations. The colonial mission has little to substantiate claims that it ever attempted to harness the missionary power of any other subordinate group in evangelizing the world.

In conclusion I would add a few theoretical remarks. The participation in mission, in a true biblical sense, is not done only on our own initiative; it is a way of participating in the humanity and activity of God. It challenges us to do mission and theology in styles different from our own. It never deteriorates into a one-sided frame of reference or slips into a partisan methodology. It calls us to reflect on missiology in biblical praxis and hence it takes into account the needs, the cry and the struggles of the people as well. In that process it breaks down the specific concerns of parochial theology and fixational ideology.

An authentic Christian missiology, like biblical theology, is concerned with the problems of human beings. It will not approach people, and culture with preconceived notions around which a theology is formed.[344] Christianity that was presented to the people in India as an alternative religion to deliver them from a degraded social position and superstitious religious background could have made a lasting impact on the political and ecclesiastical circle, if only the mission had taken the liberation struggle of the people

343. Ibid.
344. See Mary Daly, *The Church and the Second Sex* (New York: Harper and Row, 1968), pp. 147-48.

seriously.[345] Such an influence could have more readily integrated Indian Christians into the newly emergent Independent India, and added their voice to nation-building. Christianity would have been viewed by non-Christians as more than a colonial vestige.

If the missionaries had attempted to contextualize the message by identifying themselves with the freedom movement and daily struggles of the people, the colonial mission would have become vulnerable and powerless by worldly standards. It would have shed all the vestiges of "triumphalism" in which it carried out its mission and made a new beginning– the ongoing revolution of liberation and freedom which was part of God's plan for the people in India.

---

345. See J.Glazik, "The Mission of the Church in Today's World," *International Review of Missions,* 56 (1967), pp. 316-29.

BIBLIOGRAPHY

Bibliography

Adams, Daniel J. *Cross-Cultural Theology,* (Atlanta: John Knox Press, 1987).

Adler, Robert. *Western Missions,* (London: Longman, 1842).

Ambedkar, B.R. *Thoughts on Pakistan,* (Bombay: Thalker & Co., 1941).

Arendt, Hannah. *The Origins of Totalitarianism,* (New York: Harcourt Brace Jovanovich, 1973).

Arnold, Matthew. *Culture and Anarchy,* ed. J.Dover Wilson (Cambridge University Press, 1969). .

Barth, Karl. *Church Dogmatics,* tr. G.T.Thompson (Edinburgh: T. & T. Clark, 1936).

--------------. *Christ and Adam: Man and Humanity in Romans,* tr. T.A.Smail (New York: Collier, 1962).

Beaver, R. Pierce. *Ecumenical Beginnings in Protestant World Mission - A History of Comity,* (New York: Thomas Nelson & Sons, 1962).

Brandell, Fernand. *On History,* trans. Sarah Matthews, (Chicago: The University of Chicago Press, 1980).

Bright, John and Rogers, J.E.T. eds. *Speeches on Question of Public Policy by Richard Cobden* (London, 1870).

Bruce, F.F. *Traditions Old and New* (Exeter: Paternoster Press, 1970).

Carey, William. *Memoir,* (Boston: Gould, Kendell, and Lincoln, 1836).

--------------. *An Enquiry into the Obligations of Christians to Use Means for the Conversion of the Heathen,* (Leicester, 1792).

Clark, N.G. *Missionary Comity-Methods and Means For Carrying Forward the Work in Foreign Field,* (Boston: American Board of Commissioners for Foreign Missions, 1886).

Cohen, Paul A. *China And Christianity: The Missionary Movement And the Growth of Chinese Antiforeignism 1860-1870,* (Cambridge: Harvard University Press, 1974).

Collier, Price. *The West in the East,* (New York: Charles Scribner's Sons, 1911).

Conference On Missions Held in 1860 at Liverpool, (London: Nisbet, 1860).

Cordier, Henri. *The Book of Marco Polo, the Venetian, Concerning the Kingdoms and Marvels of the East,* tr. and ed. Sir Henry Yule, (London: J.Murray, 1920).

Curtin, Philip D. ed. *Imperialism* (New York: Walker and Company, 1971).

Coupland, Sir Reginald. *Raffles,* (London: Oxford University Press, 1926).

Cullman, Oscar. *Immortality of the Soul or Resurrection of the Dead? The Witness of the New Testament?* (London: Epworth Press, 1959).

Daly, Mary. *The Church and the Second Sex,* (New York: Harper and Row, 1968).

Daniel, Norman. *Islam, Europe and Empire,* (Edinburgh: The University Press, 1966).

Delavignette, Robert. tr. by J.R.Foster, *Christianity and Colonialism,* (New York: Hawthorn Books, 1964).

Dharker, C.D. ed., *Lord Macaulay's Legislative Minutes* (London, Oxford: Oxford University Press, 1946).

Dreyfus, Hubert L. and Rabinow, Paul. *Michel Foucault: Beyond Structuralism and Hermeneutics,* (Chicago: The University of Chicago Press, 1983).

Embree. A.T. *Charles Grant and British Rule in India* (London: 1962).

Fannon, Frantz. *The Wretched of the Earth,* trans. Constance Farrington, (New York: Grove Press, 1963).

Ferber, Holden. *John Company at Work,* (Cambridge: 1951).

Feuerbach, Ludwig. *The Essence of Christianity,* trans. George Eliot (New York: Harper Torchbooks, 1957).

Fieldhouse, D.K. *The Colonial Empire: A Comparative Survey From the Eighteenth Century,* (New York: Delacorte Press, 1967).

Firth, Cyril B. *An Introduction to Indian Church History,* (Madras: CLS, 1961).

Foucault, Michel. *The Archaeology of Knowledge,* (New York: Pantheon Press, 1972).

------------. *The Order of Things: An Archaeology of Human Science,* (New York: Vintage/Random House, 1973).

------------. *Discipline and Punish: The Birth of the Prison,* trans. Alan Sheridan, (New York: Vintage/Random House, 1979)

------------. *The History of Sexuality,* trans. Robert Hurley, (New York: Vintage/Random House, 1980).

------------. *Madness and Civilization: A History of Insanity in the Age of Reason,* trans. R.Howard (New York: Vintage/Random House, 1973).

Gandhi, Mahatma. *His Own Story,* ed., C.F.Andrews, (New York: The Macmillan Co., 1930).

--------------. *Young India 1919-22,* (New York: B.W.Huelisch Inc., 1923), p.11.

Geffre, Claude. *The Risk of Interpretation: On Being the Christian Tradition in a Non-Christian Age,* tr. David Smith, (New York: Paulist Press, 1987).

Graham, Carol. *Azariah of Dornakal,* (London: SCM, 1967).

Grant, Charles. *Observation of the State of Society Among the Asiatic Subjects of Great Britain, Particular With Respect to Moral and Means of Improving It,* (Privately Printed, 1792).

Grant, Jacquelyn. *The Kairos Covenant,* ed. Willis H. Logan, (New York: Friendship Press, 1988).

Gustafson, James. *The Church as Moral Decision-Maker,* (Philadelphia: Pilgrim Press, 1970).

Habermas, J. *The Theory of Communicative Action: Reason and the Rationalization of Society,* tr. T.McCarthy, (Boston: Beaver Press, 1984).

Hay, Danys. *Europe: The Emergence of an Idea,* 2nd ed. (Edinburgh: Edinburgh University Press, 1968).

Heschel, Abraham J. *The Prophets* (New York: Harper & Row, 1962).

Hesselgrave, David J. *Communicating Christ Cross-Culturally,* (Grand Rapids: Zondervan, 1978).

Hollis, Michael. *Paternalism and the Church,* (London: Oxford University Press, 1962).

Holmes, Arthur F. *Faith Seeks Understanding: A Christian Approach to Knowledge,* (Grand Rapids: William B. Eerdmans, 1971).

Howse, Ernest Marshall. *Saints in Politics,* (Toronto: University of Toronto Press, 1952).

Hugh, James, *The History of Christianity in India,* (London: Seeley and Bernside, 1839).

Jameson, Frederic. *The Political Unconscious: Narrative as a Socially Symbolic Act,* (Ithaca, New York: Cornell University Press, 1981).

Johnson, James. ed. *Report of the Centenary Conference on the Protestant Missions of the World,* (London: James Nisbet, 1888).

Kabbani, Rana. *Europe's Myths of Orient,* (Bloomington: Indiana University Press, 1986).

Kaye, John W. *Christianity in India: An Historical Narrative,* (London: Smith, Elder & Co., 1859).

Khan, Shafaat Ahmad. *The East India Trade in the Seventeenth Century in its Political and Economic Aspects,* (London: Oxford University Press, 1923.).

King, David. *The State and Progress of Jamaica,* (London: 1850).

Kling, Blair. *The Blue Mutiny,* (Philadelphia: University of Pennsylvania Press, 1966).

Knorr, Klaus E. *British Colonial Theories,* (Toronto: University of Toronto Press, 1944).

Koyama, Kosuke. *Water Buffalo Theology* (London: SCM, 1974).

------------. *Mount Fuji and Mount Sinai,* (New York: Orbis Books, 1984).

Kuriakose, M.K. *History of Christianity in India: Source Materials* (Madras: CLS, 1982).

Latourette, Kenneth S. *History of the Expansion of Christianity,* Vol. III, (New York & London: Harper and Row Bros., 1939).

------------. *History of the Expansion of Christianity,* Vol.V (New York & London: Harper & Row Bros, 1943).

Laurie, David. *Hints Regarding the East India Monopoly,* (Glasgow: R. Chapman Printed for Gale Curties, 1813).

Levi-Strauss, Claude. *The Savage Mind,* (Chicago: The University of Chicago Press, 1966).

Lochhead, David. *The Dialogical Imperative,* (New York: Orbis Books, 1988).

Luzbetak, Louis J. *The Church and Cultures,* (Techny, Illinois: Divine Word Publications, 1963).

Macaulay, Thomas Babington. *Complete Works,* (London: Longman, 1866), Vol. XI.

Mahmood, Syed. *A History of English Education in India 1789-1893,* (India, Aligarh, 1895).

Majumdar, A.K. *Advent of Independence,* (Bombay: Bharatya Vidya Bhavan, 1963).

Majumdar, R.C., ed., *British Paramountcy and Indian Renaissance,* (Bombay: Bharatiya Vidhya Bhavan, 1965).

Mayhew, Arthur. *Christianity and the Government of India,* (London: Faber & Gwyer, 1931).

Marshall, P.J. *Problems of Empire: Britain and India 1757-1813,* (London: George Allen & Unwin Ltd., 1968).

McCully, Bruce Tiebout. *English Education and the Origins of Indian Nationalism,* (Gloucester, Mass: Peter Smith, 1966).

Metcalf, Thomas. *The Aftermath of Revolt - India, 1857-1870* (Princeton, N.J.: Princeton University Press, 1964).

Mill, James. *The British History of India,* (London: Baldwin, Cradock and Jay, 1820).

Mill, John Stuart. *Dissertation and Discussion: Political, Philosophical and Historical,* (Boston: Wm. V.Spencer, 1864).

--------------. *On Liberty and Representative Government,* 2nd. ed. (London: J.W.Parker & Son, 1838).

Mittal, S.K. *Peasant Uprisings and Mahatma Gandhi in North Bihar,* (Meerut: Anu Prakasan, 1978).

Moraes, George M. *A History of Christianity in India, A.D.52-1542,* (Bombay: Manaktalas, 1964).

Moon, P. *Reflections on British India,* (Delhi: Durga Publications, 1984).

Moore, R.C. *Spread of Christianity,* (Chicago: University of Chicago Press, 1919).

The New Delhi Report of the Third Assembly of the W.C.C.1961, (London: SCM, 1962).

Neill, Stephen Charles. *The Cross Over Asia,* (London: The Canterbury Press, 1948).

--------------. *Colonialism and Christian Missions,* (London: McGraw Hill Book Company, 1966).

--------------. *The Story of the Christian Church in India and Pakistan,* (Grand Rapids, Mi: Wm. B. Eerdmans Publishing Co., 1970).

----------------. *History of Christianity in India,* (Cambridge: Cambridge University Press, 1985). Vol.II.

Neuhaus, Richard John. *The Catholic Movement: The Paradox of the Church in the Postmodern World,* (San Francisco: Harper and Row, 1987).

Niebuhr, H.Richard. *The Meaning of Revelation,* (New York: Mcmillan Co., 1947).

----------------. *Christ and Culture,* (New York: Harper Torch Books, 1956).

Nida, Eugene. *Message and Mission: The Communication of Christian Faith,* (New York: Harper, 1960).

Nussbaum, Martha. *Fragility of Goodness,* (Cambridge, New York: Cambridge University Press, 1986).

Oddie, Geoffrey, *Social Protest in India: Protestant Missionaries and Social Reforms,* 1850-1900, (New Delhi:Manohar, 1979).

Panikkar K.M. *Asia and Western Dominance,* (London: George Allen & Unwin, 1959).

Parsons, Talcott. *Societies: Evolutionary and Comparative Perspectives,* (Englewood Cliffs, NJ: Prentice Hall, 1971).

Payne, Ernest Alexander. *South-East From Serampore,* (London: The Carey Press, 1945).

Philips, Cyril Henry. *The ·East India Company,* (Manchester: Manchester University Press, 1961).

------------. ed., *Historians of India, Pakistan and Ceylon,* (London: Oxford University Press, 1961).

Pickett, J.Waskom. *Christian Mass Movements in India,* (Cincinnati: The Abingdon Press, 1933).

Proceedings of the Union Missionary Convention Held in New York, May 4th and 5th, 1854, (New York: Taylor & Hogg, 1854).

Proceedings of the South Indian Missionary Conference Held at Ootacamund, April 19th-May 5th, 1858, (Madras: SPCK, 1858).

Rapson, E.J. *Dictionary of National Biography,* ed. Leslie Stephen & Sidney Lee, (New York, 1890), Vol. XXII.

Report of the Fourth Decennial Missionary Conference Held In Madras, December 11-18, 1902, (Madras: CLS, 1903).

Robertson, E.H. *Christians Against Hitler,* (London: SCM, 1962).

Said, Edward. *The World, the Text and the Critic,* (Cambridge, Massachusetts: Harvard University Press, 1983).

------------. *Beginnings: Intention and Method,* (New York: Basic Books, 1975).

------------. *Orientalism,* (New York: Vintage Books, 1979).

Scharlemann, Robert P. *On the Other: Dialogue and/or Dialectics* (Lanham, Maryland: University Press of America, Inc. 1991).

Schwab, Raymond. *The Oriental Renaissance: Europe's Rediscovery of India and the East, 1690-1880,* tr. Gene Patterson-Black and Victor Reinking (New York: Columbia University Press, 1984).

Seymour, M.C. ed. *The Travels of Sir John Mandeville,* (London: Oxford University Press, 1968).

Shebbeare, John. *Letters on the English Nations,* 2nd. ed. (London: S. Crowder, 1756).

Silva Rego, A. Da. *Historia das Missioes do Padrado Portugues do orieente India,* Vol. 1 (Lisbon: Agencia Geral das Colonias, 1949).

Sittaramayya, *History of the Indian National Congress,* (Bombay: Patma Publications, 1966).

Smart, James D. *The Strange Silence of the Bible in the Church: A Study in Hermeneutics,* (SCM Press, 1970).

Smith, George. *The Life of Alexander Duff,* (New York: American Tract Society, n.d.).

Sophia, the Marchioness of Bute. ed., *The Private Journal of the Marquess of Hastings,* 2nd ed. (London: Saunders and Otley, 1858).

Stanley, Brian. *The Bible and the Flag,* (Leicester: Apollos, IVF, 1991).

Stebbing, Henry. *A Sermon Preached Before the Incorporate Society for the Propagation of the Gospel in Foreign Parts,*(London: E. Owen, 1742).

Stock, Eugene. *History of the Church Missionary Society,* (London: Gilbert and Rivington, 1899). Vols.I-V.

Stokes, Eric. *The English Utilitarians and India,* (Oxford: Clarendon Press, 1959).

Strausz-Hupe, Robert and Hazard, Harry W. eds., *The Idea of Colonialism,* (New York: Frederick A. Praeger, Inc., 1958).

Sundkler, Bengt. *Church of South India: The Movement Towards Union 1900-1947,* (London: Lutterworth Press, 1954).

Taylor, Mark, *Altarity,* (Chicago: University of Chicago Press, 1987).

Thekkada, Joseph. *From the Middle of the Sixteenth to the End of the Sixteenth Century (1542-1700),* (Bangalore: The Church History Association of India, 1982).

Thielicke, Helmut. *A Little Exercise for Young Theologians,* tr. Charles L. Taylor (Grand Rapids: Eerdmans, 1962).

Thomas, M.M. *The Christian Response to the Asian Revolution,* (London: SCM, 1966).

Thompson, Edward. *The Other Side of the Medal,* (New York: Harcourt, Brace and Company, 1928).

Tibawi, A.L. *British Interest in Palestine 1800-1901,* (London: Oxford University Press, 1961).

Tillich, Paul. *Systematic Theology,* (Chicago: University of Chicago Press, 1951). Vols.1-II.

------------. *Theology and Culture,* ed. Robert C. Kimball, (New York: Oxford University Press, 1959).

------------. *The Future of Religions,* ed. Jerald C. Brauer, (New York: Harper & Row, 1966).

Tracy, David. ed. *Toward Vatican II,* (New York: The Free Press, 1978).

Trevelyan, Charles E. *On the Education of the People of India,* (London: Longmans, 1838).

----------. *The Competition of Wallah,* 2nd ed., (London: 1866).

Trevelyan, George Otto. *The Life and Letters of Lord Macaulay,* (New York, 1871).

VanDusen, H.P. *One Great Ground of Hope - Christian Mission and Christian Unity,* (Philadelphia: Westminster Press, 1961).

Watt, George. *The Commercial Products of India: The Dictionary of the Economic Products of India,* (London: J. Murray, 1908).

Weber, Hans-Ruedi. *Asia and the Ecumenical Movement,* (London: SCM Press, 1966).

Weber, Max. *Caesar: The Beloved Enemy,* (London: SCM, 1955).

Williams, Raymond. *The Long Revolution,* (London: Chatto & Windus, 1961).

Woodrow, H. ed. *Macaulay's Minutes on Education in India,* (Calcutta, 1862).

Worsley, Peter. *The Third World,* (Chicago: The University of Chicago Press, 1964).

Wuthnow, Robert. *Communities of Discourse* (Cambridge, Massachusettes: Harvard University Press, 1989).

ARTICLES AND JOURNALS

Hunter, William. *The Contemporary Review,* "Islam and Christianity in India", Vol. LIII, Feb. 1888.

Philip, T.V. *The Indian church History Review,* "Christianity in India During Western Colonialism: Conflict, Reconciliation, or Adjustment," (Bangalore: The Church History Association of India, 1987).

Potts, Daniel E. *Journal of Ecclesiastical History,* "The Baptist Missionaries of Serampore and the Government of India, 1792-1813," March 1964.

Glazik, J. *International Review of Missions,* "The Mission of the Church in Today's World," Vol. 56, 1967.

The Literary Digest, LXV, (May 1920).

The Missionary Review of the World, XLI, (April 1918).

The World Outlook, VI, (July 1920).

The Literary Digest, LXIV, (June 1920).

The Nation, CX, (June 1920).

Joshi, D.L. "A Call to Indian Christians", *Church Missionary Intelligencer,* (March 1906).